D1294285

COLOR
in Hooked Rugs

by PEARL K. McGOWN

Other Books by PEARL K. McGOWN

"The Dreams Beneath Design"
"YOU . . . Can Hook Rugs"

LIBRARY OF CONGRESS CATALOG CARD NUMBER 54-10910
First Printing, July, 1954

LITHOGRAPHED IN THE UNITED STATES OF AMERICA
BY BUCK PRINTING COMPANY, BOSTON, MASS.

Dedicated to my grandchildren,

JIMMIE *and* JANE

Acknowledgment

To you, dear Teacher, I am greatly indebted for your enthusiasm and love of our craft which you have passed on for others to enjoy — and for your personal interest in each pupil's problem in achieving her desire to create color harmony in her hooked rugs — and for your cooperation in securing descriptions of the color plans, and in many instances, detailed information of dye formulas. Only YOU know the background of endeavor which underlies each rug illustrated herein, the selection of a pattern, the decision of a color plan, the gathering of materials, the dyeing of it, and the hours of patient teaching and encouragement which you are called upon to give to those who are prone to "fall by the wayside."

To you, dear pupils, who have made all the lovely rugs illustrated herein, my sincere appreciation for your graciousness in supplying descriptions of your rooms and the color plans of your choice, but most of all, for your hours of industry and perseverance necessary to create beauty in your rugs.

To my staff, who have been so helpful and patient in conducting the vast correspondence and extra work necessary to collect these facts, and to all others who have helped in any way, I am indeed grateful.

I am especially indebted to the Munsell Color Company of Baltimore, Maryland, for their full cooperation in presenting my subject, and for the loan of their Plate of Red.

And to you, dear reader, don't be confused over the word "padula" which you will not find in your dictionary. It is merely a rugger's term for any flower which cannot be identified with reality, and any color which may have been capitalized is merely to distinguish it as the name of a dye.

May this book open your mind to a new appreciation of color in everything you see.

Pearl K. McGown

Table of Contents

[v]

List of Illustrations

〜〜〜〜〜〜〜〜〜〜〜〜〜〜〜〜〜〜〜〜

List of Illustrations

List of Illustrations

*In color.

List of Illustrations

*In color.

HASKELL HALL, ATLANTIC UNION COLLEGE, SOUTH LANCASTER, MASS.,

Frontispiece

Color

Color is one of the most important subjects of the day. I know YOU have become more conscious of color through technicolor and third dimensional films. The time may be shorter than you think when we shall all take it for granted on television.

Yet it is only as you begin to USE color yourself, and apply it to some form, that you thoroughly appreciate it in all you see. The study of color is not difficult. Actually it is quite simple when you accept the fact that every color has three dimensions — its hue, value and intensity.

It is a fascinating subject! Colors may be likened to people. Some are warm and gay — others cool and retiring. Some people (like colors) have values which are light or weak, while others are deep and solid. Some people (and colors too) have weak and almost colorless personalities, while others have strong and intense characteristics.

The success of bringing either color or people together to form an interesting assembly depends upon the proportion of gaiety and warmth with those of cool and retiring nature. Too much of the former could become blatant and loud — too much of the latter could be cold and forbidding. Much depends upon the atmosphere which you wish to create in a color scheme, or at a party.

Colors, and people too, are best when their values are mixed or contrasting. Perhaps that is why so many light-hearted women marry such deep and thoughtful men (attracting their opposites!). We know, too, that the brighter and more sparkling personalities (and colors), which tend to dominate all those around them, are best when played against those people (or colors) willing to play "second fiddle."

Yet color is a scientific subject, a controversial one too, for its greatest scientists differ in their opinions. No wonder, because there are three distinct phases to the study of color.

First, from the viewpoint of the physicist who discusses the source of color, as from the wave lengths of light. That fact was discovered in 1666 when Sir Isaac Newton admitted a beam of light through a small hole into a darkened room, and when it fell upon a prism, a rainbow appeared of red, yellow, green, blue and violet. Thus sunlight, which really consists of many rays, each of which, when permitted to impinge separately upon the retina of the eye, produces the sensation of a distinct color.

Second, from the ideas of the chemist who approaches the subject through dye and pigments.

Third, from the theories of the psychologist who is concerned with the visual and emotional effects of color upon the individual.

The same laws do not apply to both pigment (such as dye) and light; therefore, what I write on color here will be based on dye. So don't be disturbed if you read many conflicting ideas on the subject of color, especially if they are based on the theory of light, for there is no attempt to reconcile the two.

We are more concerned here with learning the law and order of color, as applied to *materials*, through *dye*, and particularly how we can use them in harmony when hooking rugs. In fact you will find, after you have read this book, that many of the practical answers to your questions on color could come from experimentation and the use of dyes. Thus this study of color — your experiments on dyeing and your application of color — will all add up to a composite knowledge which will help you achieve an outlet for your own harmonious expression of color, particularly in your hooked rugs.

To successfully use color, one must understand certain rules and be able to anticipate the influence, not only of one color upon another, but the general effect upon the individual. I say "individual" rather than "people," because color is an individual matter. So we must each learn how to use it harmoniously to secure the effect we desire. Since color is a personal choice, only *you* can decide when it is pleasing to *you*.

The study of color will open your mind to a new appreciation and enjoyment of it, but it will also make you more and more selective in your choice of it, in what you use, create or observe.

The knowledge of its principles will make you also acutely conscious of its discords. (I can't bear pickled beets and red tomatoes on the same table!) However, this knowledge should spur you on to learn to use color with harmony, for once its principles and rules are understood, you may use it freely in following any creative urge, planning your color schemes with a fair certainty of the results. There is no substitute for creativeness in the use of color, so, once understood, let your rules and principles become the *tools* and not the *master* of your craft.

Now *you* may have a *natural* instinct to form harmonious color combinations in clothes, rugs or the decoration of your home. Then you are a born artist, but few of us have it without long study. In fact, many people are absolutely unaware of their *lack* of this knowledge until they begin to hook and use color. As one rugger said: "I thought leaves were just green. I never knew there could be so many different shades and tints of it."

Or you may be *afraid* to use color, only to miss its possibilities for emotional and physical reactions.

I have stressed the fact that color is an individual reaction because each of us differs from the other in his selection and appreciation of color, for each one *sees* color differently, due to his eyesight.

The fact that you may have unusually sharp vision of color permits a unique appreciation of it, for others are deprived of its enjoyment because of partial or total color blindness.

The influence of color is vital to your personality and enjoyment of life, for it affects your whole being. It has the power to "lift" or "depress" you. As used in your rugs, color may sound the keynote of interest in a room, as before a fireplace or divan. Those you select can sing a song of hospitality and fill a room with charm, or contrariwise, may be cold and depressing, or loud and discordant. Your choice of color may be influenced by past associations, or better still, from an acquired knowledge of it. Thus, your perception of color is a personal experience!

Understanding the law and order of color will enable you to combine its hues to please yourself, or those whom you must serve.

The Law and Order of Color

How can we discuss color when it is so difficult to convey our ideas to another, unless we have a sample of the particular shade or tint of which we speak? I may refer to a "turquoise blue," but it is impossible for you to know the identical color of which I speak. I may use adjectives describing it further as a "deep turquoise blue," but if I then show you a sample of it, you might possibly say: "Oh, I wasn't thinking of such a *grayed* shade of it, I thought you meant a more *intense* shade, or one of a greener cast."

But that confusion can cease. This book presents you with a way of speaking of or defining color in a language which others will understand. Every teacher and student should know this language. It is known as the Munsell system of color, established by Albert H. Munsell, Boston, Massachusetts, about 1912. He created a system which enables you to envision all color in perfect order, defining each color according to its value and intensity in a vertical scale of values and a horizontal scale of intensities, defining each one in its numerical order of both value and intensity.

This system is used and recommended by the United States Department of Agriculture, the Encyclopaedia Britannica, various color printing companies the world over, and is rapidly becoming standardized by decorators, industry and mercantile establishments. I have even seen it used in an article for physicians to define the actual color of blood.

First, let's just think of all the different colors there are. Most of us were taught the Prang system of color, which includes red, orange, yellow, green, blue and violet (six), but Munsell felt that the division in the rainbow of color is better divided into five parts than six, because orange (being a mixture of red and yellow) does not fill as large an area as each of the other five, which he refers to as the five captains of color.

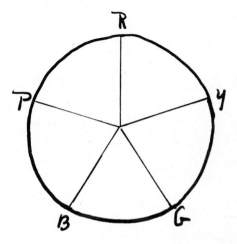

The three primaries are of course red, yellow and blue. Green is secured from a mixture of yellow and blue, and purple from a mixture of red and blue. Orange occupies a small area between red and yellow, in the section which I shall later refer to as yellow-red.

Now halfway between these five captains are five intermediary colors. Between red and yellow there is yellow-red. (That is where orange lies, as well as all shades of browns.) Between yellow and green is green-yellow; between green and blue is blue-green; between blue and purple is purple-blue; and between purple and red is red-purple. In this sketch we now have ten hues, and their names are the FIRST dimension of a color.

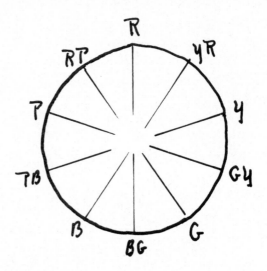

It is not necessary to write out the whole color each time you may wish to refer to it. Instead, use the first letters for abbreviations to indicate the first measurement of color, its HUE, as follows:

R	for	Red	BG	for	Blue-Green
YR	"	Yellow-Red	B	"	Blue
Y	"	Yellow	PB	"	Purple-Blue
GY	"	Green-Yellow	P	"	Purple
G	"	Green	RP	"	Red-Purple

Get their order strongly imprinted upon your mind, so you know their sequence and the relationship of each to the others.

(I will increase this family of colors later on for a still finer distinction.)

Now we have long thought of color as a flat surface, as in these sketches. From now on I want you to think of color as a solid sphere, with all hues, in their various values and intensities in perfect order, as shown on the Color Tree, page 288.

If you will study this Color Tree closely, noting the perfect law and order of all the colors, arranged as to values and intensities, it will then be easier for you to understand the three dimensions of color, as I discuss them.

Notice that all the colors grow lighter and more delicate at the top, and gradually grow darker toward the middle, with very dark shades at the bottom. You will also notice that each color grows more grayed as it nears the center, which we will call the "neutral pole," and more intense as it extends to the outer area of the sphere. Thus, each little square of color may be precisely defined as to its value and intensity. They are placed at regular, scientifically measured intervals, as definite as the keyboard on a piano. Just as a piano's keys may sound a beautiful chord of music from a rich range of *notes*, so too, colors may be combined in a chord of harmony from the rich range of definite *tones of color*.

The Neutral Pole

But at the center of this Color Tree or Sphere is a trunk or pole, which is called the neutral pole. Why? Because there is no tinge of color in it. Actually, as you will learn later, the proper mixture of any two exactly opposite colors will produce neutral gray. This neutral pole changes from black at the base, gradually growing lighter, into very dark gray, dark gray, medium dark gray, medium gray, medium light gray, light gray, very light gray and white at the top.

These varied grays are scientifically exact too, by measurement of a photometer, and are given numbers to show their position on the neutral pole. Thus black at the bottom is 1; white at the top is 9, and all intermediate grays are numbered according to their position between these two extremes, as shown here.

NEUTRAL POLE

9
8
7
6
5
4
3
2
1

You have probably referred to these neutral grays, in all their gradations, as pure white, oyster gray, pearl gray, light gray, medium gray, dove gray, Oxford gray, Oxford black and black, but it will be clearer to others if you designate them by initials — N meaning Neutral, with the number of the value following. Thus N 1 would be black, N 5 medium gray and N 9 white.

Now again, get this Color Sphere firmly planted in your mind, so you can easily visualize this neutral pole at the center, gradually changing from Black at the base to White at the top, as the axis of the entire Color Sphere, where each wedge touching it begins to turn to a definite hue.

Values

Just as neutrals are in a scale of values, so, too, are all hues, except that a color cannot be as dark as black, and therefore starts with 2,* graduating up through 8, because it cannot be as light as white (9). Actually there are still finer distinctions in values, for you could increase them to 18, if a finer distinction were necessary. In fact, even in white there is a variation of values. I often refer to one of them as "dirty white," as different from pure white. Gather your varied white materials together and notice their differences. Thus, in dyeing, a purer color can be secured over the purest white than can one (which I usually prefer) over dirty white.

But going back to the *values* of color, notice in the Color Tree how they are lined up vertically, with the grayest ones against the neutral pole, and as they extend out horizontally, each set of vertical values grows more intense, yet all are in perfect order. This should not sound technical, because you have already been using these series of values in shading a rose from a dark to a light hue.

So value is the SECOND dimension of color, indicating

---

* The color cards used in my Color Course start with the 3rd value, since it is dark enough for all practical purposes in studying color.

its degree of lightness or darkness. You indicate the value of a color by using the value number immediately after the hue letter, thus R 2 would be the darkest value of R, and R 8 the lightest.

If you have difficulty in remembering whether your value numbers start with the bottom or top, it may help you to think of them as a scale of music, running up from deep, *low* tones (dark, low values, low numbers) to the light, high notes of music (light, high values, high numbers). If you don't play the piano, SING your *low*, dark values as you ascend the scale, into the light, *high* values, until there is no doubt that the dark values begin with the low numbers, and that the light values are high numbers.

Now look at the Color Tree again, and note that some scales of values are short because, as color becomes more intense, it has fewer values, and each color varies in this respect from others. This is because of its scientific measurement, so just accept the fact and don't worry about its reasons, for *you* are only concerned with the *practical application* of color. Besides, there is more about this feature later on.

So now you might more closely describe a very dark maroon as possibly a 3rd value (R 3), or a very light pink as a 7th or 8th value (R 7 or R 8), but you have not yet indicated whether the maroon was a *rich*, or *weak grayed* shade, or the very light pink a *grayed* or *bright* pink. So this THIRD dimension of color we refer to as its intensity.

Intensity or Chroma

Now let's look closely at the sheet of R, page 292, to get a better understanding of intensity.

Notice how each scale of values also grows more intense as it extends horizontally. Each separate color fits into its proper place, not only according to its degree of lightness or darkness, but according to its gradual intensification of color as it extends outward horizontally. Notice how each value

[9]

changes from its weakest degree of color, which lies nearest the neutral pole, to its greatest intensity, where it can become no stronger in that particular value.

These steps are also numbered, beginning with 1 for the series lying next to the neutral pole, as shown by sketch. Skips of odd numbers — 3, 5, etc. — are made because there is such a slight difference in one step that two steps are close enough for our practical purposes. Colors lying near the neutral pole, being of weak or grayed intensity, would be the low numbers (like 1 or 2). Those marked 4 or 6 would be of medium intensity, and those from 8 up would be of higher intensity (greater brilliance).

Thus, the intensity or strength of any color depends upon its position, according to the number of horizontal steps away from the neutral pole, each value changing in gradual steps, from a very weak, grayed tint or shade, to its maximum strength in that particular value.

Thus, two colors may be the same in hue (R), and the same value (neither lighter nor darker than the other), but of different intensities. For example, a medium value which you would probably refer to as a "warm gray" (R 5/1), and a bright intensity of that value which you might call "coral red" (R 5/12). (See page 292.) Thus, both are of the same value, but of different intensities. It is the intensity or strength of the color (or, practically speaking, of dye) that makes the difference. It is as though you used a tiny bit of Scarlet to warm up a medium gray material for R 5/1, and a much stronger solution of the same Scarlet dye over white in the other for R 5/12.

As each hue extends out around this Color Sphere, from its grayest (around the neutral pole), to its greatest intensity (in the outer area), each step of intensity forms ever widening circles in each series of values, anyone of which would appear like the following sketch, each circle of intensity being numbered from the lowest next to the neutral pole.

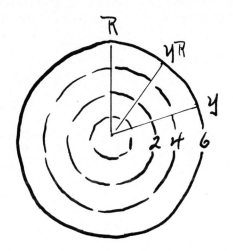

This will help you to understand why it is so easy to blend from a very grayed R which you would probably term a warm gray, into a very grayed YR, which you would probably refer to as a taupy gray., Just as these steps in the weak intensities from one hue to another are nearer together and blend easily, just so each step in the strongest intensities are further apart and do not blend as easily.

Again, you would indicate the intensity of the color by adding its number after an oblique sign (/), which follows the value number. Thus, you now have color in three dimensions — its hue, its value and its intensity. Now you could more clearly define a rich maroon as R 3/6, or a light grayed pink as R 8/2.

Now think of all the other colors in this Color Tree or Sphere, arranged in the same perfect order, their intensities keeping their own order of values vertically, their values keeping their own order of steps of intensities horizontally.

Now about this time you are going to say: "But of what use are these diagrams of color to me, when I am using various shades of materials for hooking?" The answer is that if you understand the law and order of color, you will be better able to sort your materials according to their values and intensities, so you can blend your colors together and use them in harmony. I can even hear some say: "Never mind telling me about *rules and theories* — just tell me how to use colors and put them together." Yes, I know you become impatient, but *please* first train yourself to visualize all color in its proper order, thinking and seeing each one always in its proper position — first, as to color in its proper position in this sphere; second, as to its value; and third, as to its intensity — until this Color Sphere is stamped indelibly upon your mind. Then, as one woman expressed it: "All of a sudden everything makes sense." It will to you too — with patience!

Without the 362 color chips used in the Color Course, and with the rear part of the Color Tree obscured, it is impossible for you to realize that there is a difference as to how each color varies from the others, some being much brighter in their lighter values (like yellow), while others are much brighter in their lower values (like purple-blue). So that this point may be clear to you, I am setting up the charts so you can note these differences.

R		BG	
Value	*Intensity*	*Value*	*Intensity*
8	1 2 4 6	8	1 2 4
7	1 2 4 6 8	7	1 2 4 6
6	1 2 4 6 8 10 12	6	1 2 4 6 8
5	1 2 4 6 8 10 12 14	5	1 2 4 6
4	1 2 4 6 8 10 12 14	4	1 2 4 6
3	1 2 4 6 8 10	3	1 2 4 6

YR		B	
Value	*Intensity*	*Value*	*Intensity*
8	1 2 4 6 8	8	1 2 4 6
7	1 2 4 6 8 10 12	7	1 2 4 6 8
6	1 2 4 6 8 10 12 14	6	1 2 4 6 8
5	1 2 4 6 8 10	5	1 2 4 6 8
4	1 2 4 6 8	4	1 2 4 6 8 10
3	1 2 4 6	3	1 2 4 6

Y

Value	Intensity
8	1 2 4 6 8 10 12
7	1 2 4 6 8 10 12 14 16
6	1 2 4 6 8 10 12
5	1 2 4 6
4	1 2 4
3	1 2 4

PB

Value	Intensity
8	1 2 4
7	1 2 4 6 8
6	1 2 4 6 8 10
5	1 2 4 6 8 10 12
4	1 2 4 6 8 10 12
3	1 2 4 6 8 10 12

GY

Value	Intensity
8	1 2 4 6 8
7	1 2 4 6 8 10 12 14
6	1 2 4 6 8 10 12
5	1 2 4 6 8 10
4	1 2 4 6
3	1 2 4

P

Value	Intensity
8	1 2 4 6
7	1 2 4 6
6	1 2 4 6 8 10 12
5	1 2 4 6 8 10 12
4	1 2 4 6 8 10 12
3	1 2 4 6 8 10

G

Value	Intensity
8	1 2 4 6
7	1 2 4 6
6	1 2 4 6 8 10
5	1 2 4 6 8 10
4	1 2 4 6
3	1 2 4 6

RP

Value	Intensity
8	1 2 4 6 8
7	1 2 4 6 8 10
6	1 2 4 6 8 10 12 14 16
5	1 2 4 6 8 10 12 14 16
4	1 2 4 6 8 10 12
3	1 2 4 6 8 10

You will notice that Yellow and Red-Purple are brightest, extending to 16, yet the charts of these two colors are quite different. Y, for instance, is brightest in its lightest values, and only moderately bright in its lowest values. RP is most intense in its middle values, yet still very bright in its darkest values. This may be one answer as to why you will find so many light and medium yellows of various intensities among both your materials and dyes, such as Canary Yellow, Buttercup Yellow, Gold, Old Gold, Nugget Gold, Aqualon Yellow, Maize, Ecru, Old Ivory and Champagne, and so few dyes (Bronze and

Khaki Drab) for the few dark values of yellow. This may also be one reason we have so many dyes of the medium to dark values of high intensity of R and RP–R, such as you would get from Cherry, Rose, Pink, Strawberry, American Beauty, Aqualon Wine and Magenta, with fewer in the lighter values, such as Aqualon Pink and Rose Pink.

Other points which will come to your attention are that R, YR and GY are the next brightest colors, while BGs are the least intense, according to scientific measurement. While Yellow is most intense in its higher values, and comparatively weak in its lower values, PB is just the opposite — weakest in its high values and strongest in its three lowest values.

Soon I will give you the names of dyes and show you where they belong in this Color Sphere, so you may have an early understanding of the relationship between the Color Sphere and your dyes.

As you ponder the above facts, it will help you understand the difference in the various hues, their varied gradations of values and degrees in intensities. As you study color further, you may run into diagrams which do not quite agree with the above. Don't be disturbed over this either, because the intensities of color have been strengthened since the Munsell system started, and may yet be strengthened further as Science develops and time goes on. The main thing is to understand that one hue does differ from another — that the change of value is in orderly vertical steps from dark base to light top — and that each orderly gradation of values increases in intensity horizontally from the weakest (near the center neutral pole) to the brightest at the outer area.

So now you have the three dimensions of any color, and all three must be given to designate the hue, value and intensity (or chroma). Thus, the middle value and medium intensity of R would be written R 5/5.

How Do You Apply These Facts?

You may wonder why I refer so often to writing the hues,

values and intensities of a color. Well, from now on — if you are really getting anything from this book — you are going to make notes of colors which intrigue you (for future reference), and you can describe these colors by their three dimensions. You will find yourself automatically reducing any material to its *general* hue, *general* value and *general* intensity when hooking rugs. You will be saying, as you hook: "Now this red is too weak; it needs more intensity or possibly a lighter value." Or, when you are blending from red to yellow-red (the two being neighbors), you will be saying: "My R must be of the same value and intensity as my YR where the two meet, if I am to make a smooth transition." You will know you can do it if they are in the same identical position in the two hues, as shown on these sketches.

v		R						
8	1	2	4	6				
7	1	2	4	6	8			
6	1	2	4	6	8	10	12	
5	[1]	2	4	6	8	10	12	14
4	1	2	4	6	8	10	12	14
3	1	2	4	6	8	10		

v		YR						
8	1	2	4	6	8			
7	1	2	4	6	8	10	12	
6	1	2	4	6	8	10	12	14
5	[1]	2	4	6	8	10		
4	1	2	4	6	8			
3	1	2	4	6				

But you will also realize that this transition is made easier when the intensities are moderate or weak, than when they are extremely bright intensities.

Likewise, you will really understand that R of medium value but rather *high* intensity (R 5/12), which you might call "scarlet," will not slide into R of medium value and *low* intensity (R 5/1), which you might term a "warm gray," because the latter will appear strikingly grayed against the intensity of the former. (See page 292.) The jump from 12 to 1 in the intensity figure instantly establishes this fact to you, or to those with whom you are discussing color.

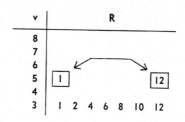

Yes, it is a new language of color, and you will not only talk it to yourself, trying to get at the root of your color problems — but also to others. You will find yourself analyzing certain colors that appeal to you, and making notes of them. It will help you convey your ideas on color to others, and it helps you too in writing me of your color problems.

So, when you look at materials, try to mentally classify their values and intensities. Define them as a *yellow*-green or *blue*-green of a definite *light, medium* or *dark* value, of a definite *brilliant, moderate* or a *weak* intensity. Doing this constantly with your materials will help tremendously in giving every hue its other two dimensions. As you use color, you will immediately find yourself realizing when and why a color is not right to achieve the effect you desire.

So keep the Color Sphere in your mind always. Become thoroughly familiar with the sequence of the colors around the sphere and visualize all those light tints at the top, dark shades at the bottom, weak intensities around the neutral pole, and strong intensities in the outer area.

HUE, VALUE and INTENSITY — always three dimensions! Oh, it's going to make you *so* color conscious, and color will become increasingly important every day.

But There Are Many More Colors Than These!

Now the ten-hue circuit is the simplest color division possible. It is only a skeleton of the entire Color Sphere! Still lacking are thousands and thousands of colors you may be seeking. You will naturally wonder where they fit into this picture. I do want you to see color as a solid sphere before we go further.

Now that you have learned this skeleton force of ten hues, and understand how each hue has its own scale of values and intensities, it is going to be much easier for you to understand that all of the ten hues may be broken up into still finer distinctions.

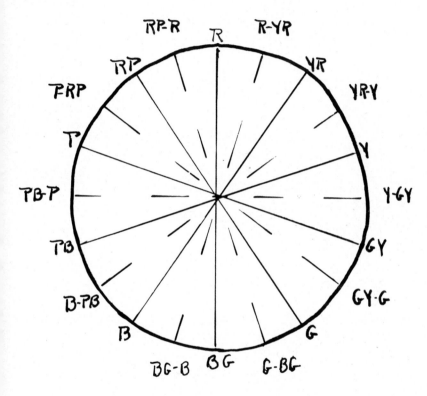

For instance, in this sketch an additional ten colors lie in equal distances between each of these ten hues. These are called "second intermediaries," and are referred to also as "three-lettered hues." Thus, we define a red that is half way between R and YR as a *red* yellow-red (emphasis on the *red*) to describe the YR. On the other side of red, half way between it and RP, we have *red purple*-red, with emphasis on the *red*

[17]

purple, for it also describes the red. By your own emphasis you have given this hue a finer distinction. All around the wheel each space half way between the major hues becomes a similar three-letter hue, to give it additional description, as follows:

R–YR	for	Red-Yellow red
YR–Y	"	Yellow red-Yellow
Y–GY	"	Yellow-Green yellow
GY–G	"	Green yellow-Green
G–BG	"	Green-Blue green
BG–B	"	Blue green-Blue
B–PB	"	Blue-Purple blue
PB–P	"	Purple blue-Purple
P–RP	"	Purple-Red purple
RP–R	"	Red purple-Red

Thus, you now have twenty hues — ten major hues and ten second intermediaries. (Since we do not use the latter as frequently as the ten major hues, note they are set out further from the circle.)

Remember now to always give emphasis to the first half of these three-letter hues, to make them more descriptive. When the first is a two-letter hue, like Yellow-red, drop its hyphen and use it instead to join the two hues, like Yellow red-Yellow, and give emphasis to the first (*Yellow red*-Yellow), which will immediately bring to your mind a brownish yellow. Practice saying these three-letter hues aloud, giving emphasis where it is due. It will help you give a wider and more complete description to your colors, for as you speak it aloud, any hue takes on additional meaning.

Don't let them confuse you. *Use* them as tools to define a hue you are seeking. "No, I don't want a *Green*-Blue green (a blue-green that swings toward green) ; I want a *Blue green*-Blue (a blue that swings toward Blue-Green)." There is quite a difference, you know! You will find yourself visualizing the colors of which you speak, and it will help you to clearly define color — especially if you are a teacher — or one who has to talk color as applied to any material or object.

Each of these three-letter hues *also* has its own scale of values and intensities which fits into this Color Sphere — for they too are light at top, dark at bottom, weak and grayed at center near neutral pole and intense at the outer area of the sphere.

But That Is Not All!

There are even greater distinctions than these! Actually, the spaces between each of these three-letter hues is made up of ten sections.

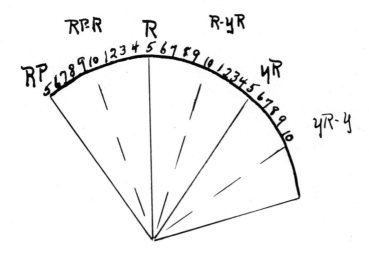

You will note in this sketch that each major hue is on the 5th or middle position. Thus, four positions precede (5) R, and four positions follow it, before reaching the three-letter hue R–YR on 10. Now each of these numbered spaces is a hue that swings slightly more toward the next major hue or the next second intermediary, as the case may be. Thus, 1, 2, 3 and 4 swing gradually away from RP–R and nearer to (5) R — and 6, 7, 8 and 9 swing gradually away from Red and nearer to (10) R–YR. This is true of every space between each of the second intermediaries.

Now again, each color on these positions 1, 2, 3 and 4, and 6, 7, 8 and 9, has *its* own scale of values and intensities just as 5 and 10 do, so they too become part of the Color Sphere. Thus, each of the 10 major hue wedges in the Color Tree on page 288 is made up of a series of ten smaller wedges, the tenth one always forming the three-letter hue or second intermediary.

Some of the colors with which you are most familiar may be in these sections. For instance, brilliant scarlets and Turkey reds! Where do they lie? They do not appear on the sheet of R, page 292. Well, the nearest to scarlet on page 292 is R 4/14, but I find that a more brilliant scarlet is just beyond middle R, in the area between R and R–YR, and would be called 6 R 4/16, a little more toward what you might refer to as an orange-red, and two steps brighter than R 4/14.

Turkey Red just precedes R–YR (9 R 5/16), swinging even further toward what you might call an orange-red, one value lighter, but of the same brilliance as scarlet. Just to show how they fit into the Color Sphere, look at the following diagrams and notice that all three are very near the same position around the Color Sphere, as checked:

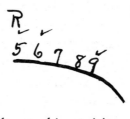

and are of similar values and intensities as shown on the following sketches. Scarlet (6 R 4/16) and Turkey Red (9 R 5/16) are a bit more intense, but very near the same value as 5 R 4/14.

v		(5)R 4/14							v		(6)R 4/16						
8	1	2	4	6					8	1	2	4	6				
7	1	2	4	6	8				7	1	2	4	6	8			
6	1	2	4	6	8	10	12		6	1	2	4	6	8	10	12	
5	1	2	4	6	8	10	12	14	5	1	2	4	6	8	10	12	14
4	1	2	4	6	8	10	12	[14]	4	1	2	4	6	8	10	12	14 [16]
3	1	2	4	6	8	10			3	1	2	4	6	8	10		

v									
8	1	2	4	6					
7	1	2	4	6	8				
6	1	2	4	6	8	10	12		
5	1	2	4	6	8	10	12	14	16
4	1	2	4	6	8	10	12	14	
3	1	2	4	6	8	10			

NOW can't you see where all the thousands and thousands of colors, in their various values and intensities, fit into a Color Sphere?

The color chips used in my Correspondence Course, shown on the Color Tree, page 288, are based on position 5. While limited to 362 colors, they suffice to teach the law and order of color. Once you understand that (like your tables of mathematics), you drop your tables and rules and begin to apply the principles. If it ever becomes necessary to be very exact, or you needed to interpret some particular notation of color, you would then understand that when a number precedes the hue, it indicates the steps toward or away from your middle (5) hues. Thus, middle R would be written 5 R and then follow with the value and intensity, but for general practice, it is assumed, if no number precedes the hue, that it is on the middle position (5) and the number is omitted.

Practice writing colors by their hue letters, value and intensity numbers. You will constantly run into these descriptive letters and numbers, if dealing with color. For instance, they are used in Elizabeth Burris Meyers' "Color and Design in Decorative Arts" in defining certain color schemes for interior decoration. You will also find them in use in many other publications. In fact, I have been besieged by those who have taken the Color Course to use these letters and numbers to define the colors of the formulas in the Dye Dabbler, and even *you* may wonder why I haven't. The reason is that while many of my readers have studied color, others have not, and my instructive pamphlets and publications must be in the general terms understood by the *average* reader. Thus, the Dye Dabblers were written with as simple and clear a description of color as it was possible for me to use. Furthermore, some of the colors suggested would not be found within the 362 color card skeleton of my color course.

From a practical point of view, this discussion of the law and order of color is for the purpose of *understanding* color in its three dimensions. Once this takes place, the average rugger will be concerned mostly with combining hues according to their *general* position and their *general* values and intensities.

Now don't jump ahead too fast — take time to think this Color Sphere through before reading further. Another thing, don't consume too much at once, but thoroughly get what you do read. Go back and review former chapters. As you read, more and more will clear up in your mind. So go over it again and again until that sphere is so clear in your thought that there is no doubt as to sequence of the hues which form it, the scale of values which makes the entire sphere light at the top (tints of the hues), dark at the bottom (deep, heavy shades), weak grayed tones around the neutral center pole and strong intensities in all the hues around its outer area.

Cool and Warm Families

All colors are divided in warm and cool families. Those from R to YG are of the warm family, while those from BG to P are of the cool family. RP and G are on the "fence," between the two. Why? Because G is made up of B (cold) and Y (warm) and therefore lends no more warmth or coolness in any color scheme. The same is true of RP, it being made of R (warm) and P (cool).

As you work with color, you must always recognize the ability of these two families to warm up, or cool off, your color harmonies. Thus, you would balance a large amount of warm colors with a smaller amount of cool ones; or vice versa, a large amount of cool colors with a small amount of warm hues, depending upon the feeling you want to get into your color scheme. You *do* get certain reactions from the colors you

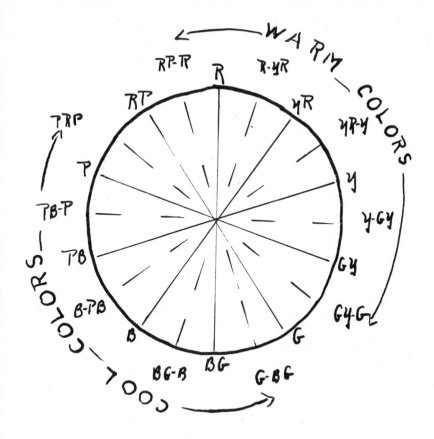

choose. The color scheme of a room, for instance, is often important, if it is desired to warm up a northeast room, or to cool off one with southern exposure.

Warm hues may be used to stimulate and cheer, or add spice and life to a room. Cool colors will prove restful and soothing, and will also give a pleasantly refreshing effect. But watch out that these cool color schemes do not become cold and depressing! In any room well balanced with both warm and cool colors, balance the colors in your rugs likewise.

Advancing and Receding Colors

These warm and cool families have another effect upon you. The warm colors are inclined to advance and seem *near*

[23]

to you. The cool colors will appear to *recede* and seem further from the eye.

It is because of the physical reaction within yourself, as the color rays are registered on your eye, that makes these varied hues *seem* to advance or recede. Your eye is really like a little camera. The various hues have different effects upon it. Red, for instance, registers behind the retina. The eye pulls it nearer than it actually is, to make the necessary compensation. The reverse happens with blue, for it registers in front of the retina, and the compensation adjustment is to push it back. Therefore, reds will advance and seem nearer — in fact appear larger — and blues will appear to recede and seem smaller. This is something to consider in planning a rug.

Dyeing

Dye is a medium through which to acquire all the count-less colors in their various shades and tints you desire in your rugs. Since I shall be constantly referring to dyes in discussing color harmonies, let us consider this practical angle now.

The average rugger — in fact anyone dealing in materials, especially where dye is concerned — should form a Color Wheel, transforming the names of the various hues into practical terms of the dyes used by me and my teachers.

You will note that I have grouped the following list of dyes according to the general area in which they would appear in the Color Wheel. (See pages 26 and 27.)

This list includes nine All-Fiber dyes (especially suitable for modern wools which may have some synthetic threads) marked by an asterisk of which eight are discussed in detail in Dye Dabbler #34.

You will note that I have classed them as generally light, medium or dark values, if used full strength over white. Some hues have several dyes, while others have only a few. Some dyes are rich and brilliant, and you should use them with caution. I have marked them with an "I" to indicate they are intense. Others are delicate, or tints of a color, and I have marked them with a "W" to indicate they are weak. The remainder are in varying degrees of intensity between these two extremes.

You will also note that the hues are exactly opposite their complements, thus R is opposite BG, even though the former has many more dyes than BG. This is for your reference when working with complementary harmonies which I discuss later.

A set of small samples (1" × 5") of all the 80 basic dyes, in 4 or 5 values, may be purchased, and I will give you the

Hues	Dyes	Values	Intensity
R	* Wood Rose	Lt.	W.
	Old Rose	Med.	
	Crimson	"	I.
	Scarlet	"	I.
	Turkey Red	"	I.
	Cardinal	Dk.	I.
	Maroon	"	
	Egyptian Red	"	
	Terra Cotta	"	
	Mahogany	"	
	Dark Brown	"	
R–YR	Coral	Lt.	
	Salmon	"	
YR	Champagne	Lt.	W.
	Tan	"	W.
	Peach	"	W.
	Apricot	Med.	W.
	Rust	"	
	* Brown Rust	"	
	Taupe	"	
	Mummy Brown	"	
	Light "	"	
	* Spice "	"	
	Medium "	"	
	Orange	"	I.
	Golden Brown	Dk.	
	Seal "	"	
YR–Y	Ecru	Lt.	W.
	Old Ivory	"	W.
	Maize	"	W.
	Aqualon Yel.	"	W.
	Yellow	"	
	Buttercup Yel.	Med.	I.
	* Nugget Gold	"	
	Gold	"	
	Old Gold	"	

Hues	Dyes	Values	Intensity
BG	Turquoise	Med.	
	Jade	"	I.
BG–B	Turquoise Blue	Lt.	W.
	Peacock	Dk.	I.
B	* Aqua	Lt.	W.
	Baby Blue	"	W.
	Robin's Egg	"	W.
	Aqualon Blue	Med.	
B–PB	Sky Blue	Med.	

* The names of the dyes referred to here are those which I have found best to date, and may be secured from me or my teachers. Since Science is

Hues	Dyes	Values	Inten-sity	Hues	Dyes	Values	Inten-sity
Y	Lemon	Lt.		PB	Lt. Blue	Med.	
	Canary	"			Blue	Med.	
	Bronze	Dk.			Copen. Blue	Dk.	I.
	Khaki Drab	"	W.		Navy "	"	
Y–GY	Chartreuse	Lt.	I.	PB–P	* Royal Blue	Dk.	I.
GY	Ocean Green	Lt.		P	Violet	Med.	I.
	Olive "	Dk.			Lavender	"	I.
	Bronze "	"			Bright Purple	Dk.	I.
	Bright "	"			Purple	"	
GY–G	Nile	Lt.		P–RP	Orchid	Lt.	
	* Hunter's Green	Med.	I.		Plum	Dk.	
	Mint Green	"					
	Aqua Green	"	I.				
G	Reseda Green	Dk.		RP	Aqualon Wine	Med.	I.
	Myrtle "	"			Burgundy	Dk.	
					Garnet	"	
					Wine	"	
					Mulberry	"	
					Magenta	"	I.
					* Red Grape	"	
G–BG	Turq. Green	Med.		RP–R	Aqualon Pink	Lt.	W.
	Green	Dk.			* Rose Pink	"	
	Dark Green	"			Pink	Med.	I.
					Rose	"	I.
					Wild Rose	"	
					Strawberry	"	
					Cherry	"	I.
					Amer. Beauty	Dk.	I.

constantly producing better and better products, I have never accepted compensation for any recommendation of a product. Therefore, I am free to change any recommendation when I feel it is in the interests of the public.

address upon request. I suggest that all teachers, and those students who intend to make several rugs, have such a set of samples to help them choose the proper dyes in combining colors, for the moment you hold them together, your own eye accepts or rejects.

Some teachers have made sets by dividing the project up among the members of a class, or a neighborhood group. In a group of ten, each would only have to dye about nine colors to complete the set, using pure white strips of 2" × 20", which may later be torn into ten 1" × 5" strips.

I strung mine loosely on a fine wire, in the same order as given here and can move them about as I wish, bringing the various colors together to form my harmonies. I turn to them constantly for answers to dye problems.

Dyeing is not hard work, nor need it be messy. I have heard my teachers say they have often given a dye lesson with their suits and furs on, to show it can be done without any muss or fuss. The result is most rewarding, and you will learn more about color from dyeing than in any other way I know.

Another experiment, which is particularly helpful to those who are teaching, is to make up a second set of swatches of combined dyes, swinging all around the Color Wheel. This can be more or less of your own choice. Pick up, for example, one of the dyes in the red section and mix with a smaller quantity of a dye two hues away, keeping in mind, of course, that the dyes ought to be fairly well balanced according to intensity, in order to have any result in the final effect. That is, don't use either a very light with a very strong dye, because the light one would probably be absorbed by the stronger one, unless you used the light one first, with only a very small amount of the strong one. For instance, a large amount of Peach — with a very little Cardinal.

Teachers, and pupils too, will find a Dye Color Wheel most helpful in determining what colors to use together.

I recommend using a good-sized cardboard for the Dye Wheel, probably 18" to 24" square, so there will be plenty of room in which to work. Draw a large circle and divide it into 20 equal areas, setting the initials of the 20 hues around the outer area, as on sketch on page 17.

Now set the names of the various dyes into the proper section of the Color Wheel in which they belong, according to the list just given you. You can add the letter "L," "M" or "D" in parentheses after each dye to indicate its value, and also the letter "I" or "W" where I have given it to you, as a caution that it is either extremely intense or weak.

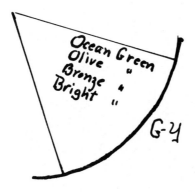

Some teachers have cut out the color and name of these dyes from the sample dye card, and used them in these Color Wheels. The only difficulty is that the color is sometimes misleading, as it is practically impossible to print the exact color of the dye itself.

There are many other ways of developing Color Wheels which are of great help, especially to teachers. One way is to dye all the colors and place them around the outer area. Or, if you want to show the difference between the intensity and the grayed shades, as shown on the Color Tree, dye the colors used in the outer area of full strength dye, and dye a few of them over light gray for the intermediate area, and still fewer in extremely weak solutions over medium light gray, so the result is extremely grayed for the area around the center neutral pole. Of course, it is not possible to use all the dyes in these two smaller areas. But you would have when completed, let us say, all the hues in the outer area in full intensity, grayed shades of some of the hues in the intermediate area and extremely grayed shades of a few around the center pole.

Of course, I would not advise you to mix dyeing with another occupation simultaneously, like one rugger who had admired the American Beauty roses which another pupil was making, and hurried home to dye some just before dinner. This rugger's husband was particularly fond of pork chops. However, it was wartime and meat was rationed. They had been saving coupons for many days to get enough together to buy the pork chops. And this was the eventful day! Nevertheless, full of enthusiasm, she first put on her pot of American Beauty dye for her roses, and then went about to prepare her dinner. The precious chops went into a pan beside the dyepot, and off she went to see about setting her table. Of a sudden, she heard a sizzling noise on the stove and turned to find that the American Beauty dye had boiled over into her pan of chops! She dashed to the sink and scrubbed furiously, but could not remove all the bright red dye. However, no more meat could be secured under the circumstances, and the chops went back on the stove. She fretted and worried until dinner time, wondering how she was going to break the news to her husband. When they sat down to dinner, she started in by saying apologetically: "I am so sorry, dear, that the chops look so pink," and he interrupted her, saying: "What do you mean, pink? Good pork chops always look pink! I think they're darn good chops!" The explanation ceased.

The methods of dyeing have been fully set forth in my publication "The Rainbow in Rags," and in back issues of the Dye Dabbler. The latter deals with a particular pattern and provides formulas for dyeing a certain color harmony for the pattern, with instructions on how to apply it. They are available at 25¢ each. Since considerable help may be secured from these two publications, I will discuss here only additional information.

Besides salt, white vinegar and acetic acid (the latter may be purchased at a drug store) are good for mordants to set the color. Use about four teaspoonfuls to a quart of water. Avoid brisk boiling, a gentle simmer (so the water smiles rather than giggles) for 30 minutes is much better for the material.

Since many materials have been treated for moisture or wrinkling you may find they will not absorb the dye. This comes to your attention when you cut the materials and find a whitish effect popping up in your hooking. There are two ways of combating this. One way is to first soak the material in a detergent and rinse well before dyeing. (The use of detergent before dyeing will always make materials absorb ordinary dye more quickly.) The other way is to use an all-fiber dye.

One word of caution in all your dyeing. Be wary of a heavy hand in the use of dye! You will be amazed at how little dye it takes to get the colors you desire, unless you are seeking the heavy, rich shades. It is better to add a tiny bit more dye than to find you have used too much. Be very STINGY with it, as though each grain was worth a dollar!

There is also a certain advantage to diluting your package of dye (1 package to 1 cup of boiling water), boiling ten or more minutes. This boiling is quite necessary to thoroughly dissolve all the ingredients which make up each particular color. Put away in tightly covered mayonnaise jars with labels of the dye. Then spoon it out very gingerly into your dye bath (plain boiling water) when ready to dye. In the South, for instance, this method is practiced because of dampness, which affects the dye.

A disadvantage would be in following the directions in the Dye Dabbler which calls for measurements of dry dye. For these measurements, a set of exact measuring spoons (1/4, 1/8, 1/16, 1/3, 1/6, and 1/12 teaspoons, available from my teachers or through me) is a necessity, in order to get the correct colors, which sometimes call for as little as a sixteenth of a teaspoon of dry dye.

Dyeing for Backgrounds

The main point to remember in dyeing for backgrounds is to get a slight fluctuation, which will develop a much more interesting background than if you get a perfectly solid shade of any one color. Therefore, never follow the directions on the package of dye. It is best to crowd your material into your dyepot so it is packed tightly. Then your dye is apt to "take" a bit blotchy, which is desirable.

If you do not have enough of one material to dye for a background, so much the better! If the variations in the values of the materials are slight, they can all be dyed as one. Even when the variations in value are more marked, like very light value with a medium light value, they may be put into the same dyepot, especially if the color you are dyeing is a *medium* value. There is enough difference in the results in the two materials to make a very interesting background. This is the way varied light to medium blue materials were dyed a dark greenish-blue for the background of my "Bermuda" stair runner at Rose Cottage. It has been greatly admired. Dr. Maybelle Sawyers (now deceased) hooked it in an irregular manner like this:

using the varied values to form a very subtle mosaic effect to an otherwise plain background.

When dyeing for dark backgrounds, try checks, mixtures and well-covered plaids in the same dyepot. The result will be a mottled TEXTURE. Avoid large plaids that have a lot of white.

A mixture of dyes in very dark backgrounds (best over dark grays) will often carry an overtone of your color scheme. For instance, if your flowers were in the Rs, Bs and Ps, you could secure a more subtle background if you added a small amount of two of the dyes to the one which you wish to predominate. For instance, add a small amount of a blue and a purple to red dye if you want a very dark red background. The background would then have a closer relationship to the flowers.

Other ways of changing color in materials you wish to use for background are by simmering it in sudsy water, or with ammonia, to lighten the value, and oftentimes to change the color too, or by removing the color with Color Remover. A report of this method is given in detail in Dye Dabbler #19. There is no guarantee that all the color can be removed, or that it will come out white, but oh, the joy of seeing what you do get! One of the most interesting backgrounds I ever saw was made from twenty-odd pairs of pants put into Color Remover. Some came out creamy, some pinkish-gray, some bluish-gray, others lavender or greenish-gray. They were all mingled to give a delightful opalescent effect. Naturally you avoid such contrasts as would distract the eye when hooked. The result should be a subtle change, one that is only apparent upon close inspection.

Oftentimes a material that you have for a background may be a little bright. Remember you can always gray it down by using a small quantity of its complementary dye. One of the loveliest rugs I have ever seen had a grayed khaki-green background, which had been dulled down by a little red dye.

There are two ways of dyeing for a shadowed background where the area under a flowered center is darker than that surrounding it. The first way is to dye three or four different values of your chosen background, close enough to slide smoothly together when fingered, so there is a gradual transition from the darkest, under the flowers, to the lightest, in the area surrounding them. The second way is to dye progressively, as suggested in Dye Dabbler #7. After measuring the distance to be hooked, from the center to outer area, multiply it by three or four times. Then dye one end in the darkest value, the middle in the intermediate values, and the other end in the lightest value, being sure that each of the three overlaps the others. Then hook it in the direction of sun rays, from the center outward.

Dyeing for Scrolls

The main thing to achieve in dyeing for scrolls is a *variation* of *values* and *intensities*. If your scroll is one hue, this is made simple by using varied grays, beiges or tans in different strengths of dye, and a smaller amount of dirty white or white in extremely weak solution of dye, for your lightest values. Use checks and mixtured materials too, especially in your darker values, and it will give the added interest of texture in the development of your scroll.

Keep in mind that as a rule scrolls are not the most brilliant parts of your color development. As a rule they cover a rather large area, and the quantity of *brilliance* in the scroll would probably be small. Therefore, in planning your material, dye much more of your intermediate and softer shades than your bright or very dark or lighter values.

A casual and easy way of getting varied values for scrolls is to stagger your material. Use your stronger dye in a generous dye bath over part of your material, and after five minutes, add more material. As you notice the dye bath becoming weaker, again add more material, and when the bath is quite weak, throw in a small piece of white to take a tint of the color.

Another casual way of getting interesting shades for a scroll is to mix your colored materials and varied textures, thus putting both plain and mixtured materials of several colors, such as blues, greens (except Kelley) and golds in the same bath. This will produce fascinating colors, and you will find them easy to work with. I would not deprive you of the fun of creating your own combinations, by limiting you to a few suggested dyes over these materials, for *creating* your *own colors* by experimenting, is part of the fascination of dyeing. This method will bring unrelated colored materials together in harmony, through a common dye bath.

Another way to dye for scrolls is by the progressive method, which I gave you in Dye Dabbler #7, where you dye one end of your material in one dye, letting the remainder hang over the top in another pan near by. Then change and immerse the middle of the strip in a second color, with both ends out of the dyepot; then change again and dye the other end in a third and lighter color. Be sure each color overlaps the next. Some consideration must be given as to the choice of these three dyes. The first should be the darkest, the second of medium value, and the last of the lighter value. Lillian Knight, member of Hookrafter's Guild, used a sequence of very dull purple, a medium bronze and a soft corny yellow, with delightful effect. She found the strips should be about three times the length of the detail she was working on.

Of course, your spot-dyeing is excellent for scrollwork. It aids in blending from one hue into another. Sometimes very casual spotting of your color onto your material after it is in the dyepot would produce some interesting effects, quite suitable for scrollwork. If you are tying up to a definite color scheme, where a close control is necessary, then I would advise you to spot your material before putting it in the dye bath. In that case, wring it out well, lay it on your sink board and spot it in much the same way you wish it to appear in your scroll. That is, if you were using three hues, like green, bronze and gold or yellow, you would probably shade the scroll from the darker values of green (in which case you would use a strong dye for spots on that end), a medium value for the second spots of bronze and the lighter values of the gold or yellow for the third spots, allowing an inch or two between the spots so the dye can spread somewhat and meet the other, to make the transition. Naturally, some consideration must be given to the general length of the area in the scroll where you are to use this transition from one hue to another. Then make the strip from three to four times as long as the detail. Roll it up tightly lengthwise and lay your rolls in a flat pan, either on a wire rack or a double thickness of paper towelling, and put only a small amount of boiling water in the bottom of the pan over your burner so it will form steam. Cover the top of the pan tightly with several thicknesses of newspaper and steam for 30 minutes. In this case, add your vinegar to your dye before you spot the material.

A third method is casserole dyeing, which I gave you in Dye Dabbler #35. This is a method of putting a layer of your darker material into the bottom of the bath, in a strong solution of the desired color and spotting with a second dye (have only a small amount of dye bath so material sticks up beyond it), then placing a second layer of material on top of it and spotting with a weaker solution of the second dye and also a third dye, and then adding a third layer of material and spotting with a weaker solution of the third dye and also a *very* weak solution of a fourth dye. Cover tightly and steam for 30 minutes. It cooks much like any casserole dish, and the color from the first layer of material will soak somewhat into the second layer, the second into the third and this brings all three together in harmony. Of course, much depends upon your CHOICE of the four dyes, and you will find analogous colors flow together best. Delightful for scrolls!

So many times I will hear ruggers say: "I think scrolls are so difficult. I never know how to handle them." If you will keep the neighboring hues in mind when dyeing for scrolls, you can pick up some very lovely combinations of color by dyeing various values and intensities of *neighboring* hues, and then applying them in such a manner as to develop one part of a scroll in one hue, blending out into knobs or curling tips of another hue. The closer the relationship between the dyes you use, the smoother will be your transition. Thus, a lovely scroll could be developed in rosy, warm browns, by combining

Rose with Rust, or Mahogany with Golden Brown, blending into rusty pinks, such as you might get from tints of Rose, Rust and Apricot. It is the combination of two or more dyes that give lovely off-shades to make a scroll more interesting.

A broad, leafy scroll must depend upon a fluctuation of values and intensities, and when two or more hues mingle, it provides more interest. This is often done through spot-dyeing material with the general colors which will produce the effect you desire. Remember, too, that when you spot-dye with two complementary colors, they gray each other down somewhat. When you hook them, the combination of the two is apt to give a much grayer effect. Spot-dyeing any beige, light gray or tan materials with Bronze Greens, Mulberry and Peach will produce some delightful scrolls, accented and emphasized by small tips or knobs of brighter Greens, with occasional broken lines of the other two colors at the edges of the scroll.

If dyeing for a painted scroll, you can get a smoother transition of your colors if you will add a small amount of one dye to another, thus carrying the hue of one over into another.

Dyeing for Leaves

Probably the simplest way of dyeing for leaves is straight gradation dyeing, that is, securing five to seven different values, so you can blend your leaf from dark to light.

A more interesting development is to dye your darkest value a *dull* shade, and each succeeding lighter value slightly brighter. Or, contrariwise, dye your darkest shade rich and gay, and in each succeeding lighter value make it slightly duller or grayer.

In dyeing for leaves, too, use two hues, starting, for instance, with a dark, dull shade of BG and grading it up to a medium value; then switching into a medium value of the same intensity of its neighboring hue, G, or even YG, getting your lighter values of the latter. Contrariwise, you may shade from a dark YG up to a light BG. These two hues may also be stepped up in intensity, or grayed down in each succeeding lighter value.

But don't be bound by reality in your dyeing. Be imaginative! Leaves may be R, such as the very grayed shades of R 3/1, R 4/1, R 5/1, R 6/1 and R 7/1. (See page 292.)

Dull leaves like these often bring out the true beauty of certain flowers. Khaki, Khaki Drab or Bronze over light tan and beige for the dark values, and tints of Bronze, Green and Old Ivory over white for highlights are also beautiful off-shades for leaves.

Even very weak Navy over medium to light values of gray, and tints of Silver Gray — or Sky Blue and Green (weak solutions) over medium and light grays, for the dark values, and Turquoise Blue over light gray and dirty white for the light values are lovely for blue leaves. Yes, you can even use very weak tints of Plum over light blue, light gray and white, where purplish-gray leaves are desired. So don't confine yourself to the reality of BG, G and YG for leaf detail!

In fact, if you dye over a series of grays, using medium dark for your shadow shades, dirty white for highlights and over medium to medium light grays for the intermediate shades, you will secure softer and lovelier colors to hook than those same dyes over white, as the latter are often much too bright. Remember, they must be very grayed if you are to use imaginative colors in leaves with colorful flowers!

Another way of dyeing for leaves is by the progressive method, described under "Scrolls." Dye one end of a strip of material in dark Reseda, the middle area in a medium Bronze Green and the other end in a light value of Bronze. In hooking, use it to shade from a dark BG base out to a light bronzy edge, or tips. In this case have your strip from three to four times the length of your line of hooking.

Dyeing for Flowers

Again, gradation dyeing works out best for the development of flowers, shading out from dark to light of one general dye. Or dye from a dark bright to a light weak — or a dark dull to a light bright highlight, as suggested under *"Dyeing for Leaves."*

Try combining two dyes for flowers. Thus dark dull values of Mahogany might blend up into lighter and brighter values of Rose Pink; or even step over into a neighboring hue, blending from dark Mahogany into a light Peach.

Experiment with mixtures of dyes to get "off-shades," such as Rust and Scarlet, Canary and Salmon, Gold and Bronze, Old Gold and Chartreuse, Aqua and Jade, Plum and Copenhagen Blue, Wild Rose and Orchid, Cherry and Maroon, using a much larger proportion of the first, with only a very small proportion of the second.

You can also get some lovely off-shades for flowers, as suggested in "The Rainbow in Rags," by putting several different pastels into the same weak dye bath. This brings them all together in a common relationship, through one dye. Doing this with various strengths of dye will give you a countless number of shades with which to work.

Dyeing for Geometrics

In dyeing for geometrics, it is usually for large areas of detail or background, or to change otherwise useless material to colors which may be utilized in this type of design.

In dyeing for the background areas, it is advisable to get a relationship in your colors to give unity to the development. Suppose you are dyeing a light grayed-green for one area of such a design, and a light grayed-tan for another area, you give them relationship by adding a little of your brownish dye to your grayed-green, and a little of your greenish dye to your brown. It does not have to be too much. Even a small amount of one dye carried over into the other will bind the two together.

Since the rule in geometrics is to use your brighter shades

in the smaller areas and details, and your softer and more grayed shades in the larger areas, one should dye smaller quantities of bright colors for accent and emphasis, and much larger quantities of the softer and grayed shades for larger areas.

In dyeing a monochromatic harmony for a geometric, an interesting effect may be secured by introducing a small amount of a neighboring hue, to pep it up. Thus, to a harmony of the many browns found in the YRs, add small amounts of Bronze or Old Gold to your dyeing. Or, on the other side of YR, add a small amount of Peach or Salmon, or even a bit of one of the reds to some of your browns. The more variations there are in the brown dyes you choose, and in their values and intensities, the better.

Dyeing for Orientals

Oriental coloring is in a class by itself. One should really study old Oriental rugs and try to secure some of the general combinations found in the antique Orientals. The colors are rich, yet subdued, and are often the "off-shades" that you cannot find in a straight dye. I have found, too, that some of the best Oriental colors, especially when applied to the larger areas of background, are secured by graying down a bright material with dye of its complementary color. Thus, some of the bright and blatant blues in medium values can be grayed down into beautiful background tones by using a weak solution of the complement of such a dye, as Spice Brown. Turkey Red materials may be grayed down with weak solutions of Peacock, or stronger solutions of Reseda Green. In fact, any of the dyes found in any two complementary colors (opposites) of your Dye Color Wheel will gray each other down. Remember that if you add too much dye, the result may be extremely grayed.

As a rule, if you are hooking an Oriental, it is to be used near real Orientals. In such a case you should plan your colors around your real Orientals, trying to obtain the same general tints and shades.

Limit yourself to a few basic colors — three is safe — but dye many different values of them. Use only one of the hues in intensity. Be sure to have real dark values as well as light ones.

Adding a small amount of one of the dyes to another will bind them more closely together and produce that sense of harmony you feel but cannot always analyze.

Remember, any color may *appear* brighter when it is massed in a large area, so control the intensity of the dye to be used for these large areas. Likewise, an extremely gay color will lose some of its gaiety when used in small areas or accents, and, therefore, must be fairly bright to accomplish your purpose.

It is, therefore, advisable to visualize the general effect you wish to achieve — and keep these points in mind during the process of dyeing.

DESIRE (A PAIR)

THE ROSES in the "Desire," hooked by Thelma Bushnell of Santa Rosa, Calif., Teacher, were made from a gradation of values of two parts American Beauty and one part Terra Cotta, with tints of Aqualon Pink for lightest values. One rose was made darker than the others by the application of more of the darker values, one of medium values and the third one was quite light. The morning glories were secured from Blue and Sky Blue dyes, most of them having light throats. Their tints were carried over into the tiny buds in the outer area of the bouquet. A marriage of the hues of both flowers (Plum) made the tulip, accented with Aqualon Pink edges. The fuchsias of Mulberry dye were a combination of the tulip and rose colors. Additional repetition was given by using some of the rose shades in the tulip, and some of the tulip hues in the morning glory. The background was a medium light beige. Bronze Green dyes were used for the tulip leaves and Reseda for the foliage of the morning glories and the two were combined for the rose leaves.

IT IS always a revelation to pupils to see how all kinds of materials and hard and harsh colors may be changed and brought into a beautiful relationship through dyeing.

"Desire," hooked by Kathryn Cogburn of Columbia, S. C., Teacher, was her experiment to teach her classes this lesson. Six reds and the same number of ugly pinks were simmered together, and then blues, lavenders and whites were added. As they took on the values desired, they were removed to a pan of water, to which vinegar was added to set the color. To complete the range of reds desired, some reds "as is" were grayed with Green dye making them very dark, almost blackish-red. The varied reds were used to develop the roses, tulips and fuchsias, giving each its own individuality by selection of values and intensities. Light grays and white were dyed in Light Blue, to which a small pinch of Rose was added for six values, and these were used for the morning glories.

For the foliage, Kelley Green was boiled to remove as much color as possible, and then grayed down with Plum and Mahogany, graying some of it more than the rest, to get a good gradation for the long tulip leaves. Four different grays were spot-dyed with Myrtle Green, Olive Green, Strawberry and Buttercup Yellow for the rose leaves. Equal parts of Olive Green and Bronze Green were dyed over gray and white for six values for the morning glory leaves.

The background utilized six different gray materials "as is" — the lightest around the floral center, gradually fingering back into darker values to an almost black at the outer edge.

"Rags to Riches," hooked by Ruth Kemp of Wellfleet, Mass., Teacher, was made for a room with pale mauve walls and a large-sized rug of deep burgundy. So the background was to tie it to her larger rug. Burgundy dye with Black added was used for an extremely dark background beneath the flowered diamonds, and for the outside border. For the smallest diamonds that form a background surrounding the larger ones, three different dye baths were used — one of Purple, one of Burgundy and one of American Beauty to which a little Burgundy was added. Into these separate baths she put all sorts and colors of materials — so they all came out into harmonizing basic colors. The darkest ones in the Burgundy or Mulberry families were used as filler for the diamonds, which were first marked off by a teal blue (Robin's Egg Blue, Turquoise Blue and a little Olive Green, the latter being repeated along the inner side of the border at the edge of the rug). There was no set plan of repetition, except to maintain a sort of rhythm, so there was a certain balance of light and dark values. Thus, two diamonds side by side might be the same value but of slightly different intensities; or they might be only slightly different in value. Occasionally one is of a brighter intensity, reflecting a bright shade from the floral detail.

From the wide variation of shades which came from the three dye baths, and the various colored materials she had put through these baths, she created a rose of rich wines and their buds of lighter values. One of the two tulips is a very grayed purple, and the other a grayed rose, both shading out to much lighter values at the tips. The iris had upper petals of pale grayed lavender, and dark plum lower petals, veined with lighter values. Some of the morning glories are purple-blue with dark throats and light funnels, but one of those at the center is a lavender white shading to slightly darker values around the center, with a light funnel. The same colors are repeated in the corner diamonds, in which she changed some of the padulas to more realistic flowers of her own choice.

TREASURED SHAWL

PERSIAN PARADISE

[46]

PROBABLY the easiest scroll to hook is one which you merely outline and fill, like "Treasured Shawl" hooked by Mrs. Harold J. King of Syracuse, N. Y., Adrienne Bradley, Teacher. Yet Mrs. King has given its simplicity a richness and interest, through the treasured Paisley shawl she used for it.

Against an outer background of black, the scroll is first outlined with a deep value of Maroon. The dark values of both outline and paisley sink somewhat into the dark background. The inner background was an old blanket of soft ivory. Only one hue and one dye were used for the floral center, Maroon being dyed into many values of rather moderate intensities. Each flower is given its own individuality by the application of values to make the roses the darkest and richest; the petunias with dark edges contrasted with dramatic light throats; the Canterbury bells of pinky whites and the lilies of white. The leaves were formed from many light and uninteresting materials which had accumulated, and were dyed with onion skins. (You will be amazed at the shades that can come from them!)

ANOTHER very simple scroll to hook is "Persian Paradise" hooked by Miss Marion Wilder of Northwood, N. H., Mary MacKay, Teacher. The simplicity of this lovely mauvy scroll comes from Purple, Maroon and blue-green dyes brushed together in the Mary MacKay style to give an overtone from both background and floral detail that delights the eye. Two shades of Gold accent its inner curve.

In the Mary MacKay method, the following were used:
Wild Rose dye blending into white for the poppies,
Maroon over gold for the iris,
Maroon over white for the petunias,
Maroon over gray for the chrysanthemums,
Purple over pink for the foxglove,
Purple and Maroon over white for the fuchsia.

The light inner background is Taupe over white, "dip-dyed" in her style, shading from dark under the floral detail to a light area around it, and is a dramatic contrast to the rich wine outer background.

No DYEING was necessary for "Maltese Cross," hooked by Mrs. Martha R. Dunlap of Harvard, Mass., Margaret Farnsworth, Teacher, who was inspired by my own "Maltese Cross" at Rose Cottage. The materials, plain, mixtured checks and plaids, are of four hues: (1) All sorts of tans and browns, (2) All sorts of greens, (3) All sorts of soft golds, (4) All sorts of rusty-reds and soft burnt orange.

Every block is outlined with dark brown, used also in the outer border. The varied tans and browns are used for the bulk of the blocks, with the other colors used for accenting lines. As an example, green is used to accent varied outlines of the geometric block, with rusty rose in the inner cross. Notice that some of the inner crosses are light with dark fillers, while others are dark edges with light fillers. Notice, too, that two rows are of much lighter values. Half the fun of hooking is playing one color against another, so the constant variation of the blocks, with the use of the same colors over and over again, gives unity to the rug as a whole. Mrs. Dunlap says: "It is a rug I can live with, and of which I'll never tire."

"Criss Cross" (left under window), hooked by Mrs. William Scott of Rochester, N. H., Mary MacKay, Teacher, has dark brown background, gold crisscross border (equal parts of Mummy Brown, Bronze and Old Gold) repeated in the trumpet flowers; tiger lily of Cardinal over gold; daisies of Maroon over yellows and purple iris blending into Mummy Brown and Yellow.

The design of "Polly," hooked by Dr. Mary B. Gillis (without benefit of teacher), was graciously offered to you through me. Her horse of rich golden browns (Mahogany, Orange and Gold over browns) is a lovely contrast to the greenish-blue sky (equal parts Silver-Gray and Peacock), and the deeper blue-greens of the grass (Myrtle and Reseda) in the foreground.

"Maltese Oriental" (under horse), hooked by Mrs. Lilli B. Cox of Winthrop, Mass., Cecile Permatteo, Teacher, is of only three hues — dull Chinese reds, greenish-blues and golds to cream — (all dyed over mixtures, beiges and dull grays), with accents of white and blackish-blue. The reds are in the wide outer border and small figures at both ends of the center; the blues are in the center background and the twisting band of outer border. All the hues and white are brought into the center detail.

"Fascination" (right under window), hooked by Lelia Bell of Riverton, Conn., Teacher, has mahogany browns predominating with Turquoise Green playing a secondary part. For contrast, the large conventional flowers are of soft reddish golds. You wouldn't recognize this rug today because it has been extended to make a six-foot hall runner!

Color Paths

〰〰〰〰〰〰〰〰〰〰〰〰〰〰〰〰〰〰〰〰〰〰〰〰〰

All color harmonies have PATHS through varied values and intensities of each hue.

Vertical Path

Let's look again at page 292. Follow any vertical path and you will recognize the varied values you now use in shading flowers. Each vertical row is all in the same intensity. Depending upon the detail you are developing, you can skip one or more values in this vertical path. When shading flowers you may wish to include all of them. A dark leaf might blend from a dark to a medium value (third to fifth values), or from a medium to a light value (fifth to seventh values). On the other hand, there are certain details which call for a more dramatic effect, such as in geometrics or Orientals. Then you skip a value or two. Therefore, in any detail needing a close shading, a continuity of values is more successful, while a more dramatic effect is secured by skips in values. An extreme contrast, for instance, in the border of a geometric detail, might skip from an extremely dark value to a medium value, and thence to a very light value. Because of the extreme *contrast* in the values, it becomes dramatic, an effect often desired in some geometrics and Orientals.

The vertical path of values which you choose makes a great difference too. Thus, if you are making a rose brighter than its leaf, you would use those vertical paths in the moderate intensities or those further from the neutral pole. The more intense, the more caution would have to be used in combining with other colors. Thus, the larger the rose, the more cautious you would become in choosing which particular vertical path of values you would use, usually avoiding those of extreme intensity.

On the other hand, on leaves you would naturally use a medium to weaker intensity of values, because as a rule, leaves are not as important, and serve only to bring out the beauty of the floral detail.

A vertical path is extremely safe, but because of its safety, possibly a bit uninteresting.

Horizontal Path

Now let's consider the horizontal path. Again notice in the plate of Red, if you followed the fourth value horizontally away from the neutral pole, all your values would be the same, but your color would change from an extremely grayed shade to a brilliant shade of the same value. There is an ever-increasing intensity in this path without any change in value. This is not the path usually chosen for floral or leaf detail, because as a rule, you need shadow and highlight for them, shadow being a *darker* value and highlight a *lighter* value.

But you could use a horizontal path to develop any flat detail which requires no depth, such as in geometrics, blending into stronger intensities for emphasis or accent.

Thus, a shell border might start with a medium value (5) of weak intensity (somewhere near the neutral pole, like R 5/2 on page 292), blending horizontally into an edge of strong intensity of the SAME value, like R 5/8.

A horizontal path is safe, but tame!

Diagonal Path

But if you take the diagonal path, you have a *change of value and intensity* each time you step up your value. Again refer to page 292, and follow a diagonal path from a dark weak

[51]

(that is, near the neutral pole) up to a light bright; or try it the opposite way from a dark bright to a light weak.

v	R						
8	1	2	4	6			
7	1	2	4	6	8		
6	1	2	4	6	8	10	12
5	1	2	4	6	8	10	12	14
4	1	2	4	6	8	10	12	14
3	1	2	4	6	8	10		

Again you can skip values as may be necessary or pleasing, to achieve the effect you desire. This continuous change of values and intensities, as you climb diagonally, produces a continuous interest for the eye, because not only the value changes, but the intensity also. If a quiet, subtle effect is desired, keep a close sequence of values and changes in intensity. You are using this path when you blend a leaf from a dark dull green base to a light bright tip. There will be many details where skips along this diagonal path will produce exciting and exhilarating effects, particularly in geometric or conventional designs.

Don't let these paths confuse you! You can use any or all of them many times in your rug. Floral or leaf detail may follow diagonal paths of dark dull to light bright, and dark bright to light weak, or conventional borders may be developed in the same manner, or in a vertical path of gradation. In certain detail such as often found in geometrics you may follow a vertical path and then go horizontally, which lightens your value and increases your intensity. Or continue again vertically, thus again lightening the value of the brighter intensity.

v	R								v	R						
8	1	2	4	6					8	1	2	4	6			
7	1	2	4	6	8				7	1	2	4	6	8		
6	1	2	4	6	8	10	12		6	1	2	4	6	8	10	12
5	1	2	4	6	8	10	12	14	5	1	2	4	6	8	10	12	14
4	1	2	4	6	8	10	12	14	4	1	2	4	6	8	10	12	14
3	1	2	4	6	8	10			3	1	2	4	6	8	10	

You can start horizontally and then climb vertically, which is growing more intense and then lightening the value of the stronger intensity, as in this sketch.

v	R							
8	1	2	4	6				
7	1	2	4	6	8			
6	1	2	4	6	8	10	12	
5	1	2	4	6	8	10	12	14
4	1	2	4	6	8	10	12	14
3	1	2	4	6	8	10		

In fact, you can combine the different values and intensities of one hue in any of these three directions, singly or together, and you will find your color blending beautifully. Just run your finger over page 292, in any or all of these directions, and you will see how one blends into the other.

These diagrams are merely to help you understand the law and order of values and intensities in the materials you use. You will soon find yourself sorting them so you can combine them perfectly.

Practically speaking, you are following the VERTICAL path when blending from dark weak to a light weak — or from dark, moderate intensity to a light, moderate intensity — or from a dark, strong intensity to a light, strong intensity.

Practically speaking, you are following a HORIZON-TAL path when blending from a dark, weak or grayed hue to a dark strong hue — or from a medium, extremely grayed hue to a medium, extremely strong hue — or from a light, very weak tint to a light, bright tint.

Practically speaking, you are following a DIAGONAL path when you blend from a dark weak or dull shadow, gradually shading it slightly lighter, and each time slightly brighter shades up to a light, bright highlight. The same is true when you blend from a dark rich shadow, gradually shading into lighter, and each time slightly weaker shades up to a light, weak highlight. Actually, dyeing a series of values in this way, so each value grows gradually lighter and brighter, or vice versa, so each value grows gradually lighter and duller, will help you establish this diagonal path in your mind.

Practice picking up your materials and folding them over your finger, to make orderly steps as suggested above, until you can form these sequences easily.

When the law and order of color is thoroughly established in your mind, you will visualize the Color Sphere with every hue in its proper place around the sphere, each having its values and intensities in perfect order — light at the top, dark at the bottom, weak at the center, and intense in the outer area. Then you are ready to study color harmony as practically applied to hooking a rug.

Now that I am ready to discuss color harmony, you must consider first the effect which one color has upon another, and also upon YOU. For there is a reaction to using or LOOKING at just ONE color.

You are probably familiar with the "afterimage" of color, and its effects upon all surrounding color. But just in case you are not, you will find that if you stare at a bright red for a minute or two and then close your eyes, or quickly shift them to something white, you will see a faint tinge of its direct opposite color, blue-green. Your eyes have become fatigued with the bright red, and they automatically seek rest in its complement. The same is true of other brilliant colors, and they may affect surrounding detail by their complements.

For this reason, if you mass a brilliant color, even in small detail in your rugs, the surrounding area may APPEAR to have a slight cast of the complementary (or directly opposite) color. Have you ever noticed that a beige, light tan or a gray material takes on a cast of color AFTER it has been hooked in? It might very likely be the afterimage of a bright color near it.

I saw a "Kent's Twig" with gay blue-green leaves in the center motif. The very light beige background beneath and around the detail had a "pinkish" cast when it was hooked. The pupil who made the rug couldn't understand why that material should appear so PINK when hooked. But I did! It was the afterimage of the gay blue-green leaves.

The effect of complementary hues upon each other, and upon surrounding background, will be discussed more fully under Complementary Harmony later.

TEACHERS' ANNUAL EXHIBIT, 1953

VERTICAL paths were probably used to create this modern and almost monochromatic "Lotus," hooked by Mrs. Paul Huffington of Bridgewater, Mass., Carolyn Cate, Teacher, although when analyzed, it appears to be an analogous harmony of YG–G and BG. It was desired to utilize odd coats, skirts, jackets, etc., and to improvise with such dyed materials as might be necessary to pull them all together. By adding the neutrals of black, oxford gray and white, together with a tweed that combined green, gray and white, a feeling of unity was secured. One of the main motifs was done with the combined neutrals in the outlines of the varied detail, with accents of yellow-green, and fillers of green, gray and white tweeds. In the second main motif, the neutrals were again used with an accent of yellow-green, but adding green and grayed blue-green. In the smaller intervening motif, more of the yellow-greens were used with only the lighter neutrals. Thus, all three motifs were closely related, and their differences lay more in the fact that each had varied areas in their design, which called for more or less of one of the materials. Something from each of the motifs was used to make the outside border, grading them in similar values. The light background was off-white.

"Blythe Shoals" (to the right) was hooked by Mrs. Kenneth W. Galencia of Worcester, Mass., Hester Bennett, Teacher. A creamy background which picked up something of the yellow from the scrolls was secured from gold wool bleached. Since the scroll was the dominating feature in this color plan, it was glamorized in many shades of yellow-greens (Bright Green, Olive Green, a speck of Black over varied gray materials for darker values, and Chartreuse over cream for light values), following the *diagonal* path from dark, dull shadows to light, bright highlights accented by tiny tips of Chartreuse. The simple floral center completed a split complementary color scheme, with purple-blues in the iris (Lavender and Purple over pale blue material), and red-purples for the tulips (Old Rose, Wine and Mulberry over pale gray and white). Repetition was given by making red-purple freckles in the creamy white foxgloves (Silver gray over cream), and by using the same greens of the scroll in the foliage detail.

Vertical paths of low intensities were used in "Garden's Gift" (to the left), hooked by Mrs. A. E. McGavin of Wyomissing, Pa., Teacher. All the flowers were white. Their shadows of gray varied somewhat — a tint of Reseda in the zinnia and a tinge of Wood Rose for turned-over petals of the magnolia, with varied green foliage. The little leafy border was four shades of blue-green (Reseda). It has an antique black background made from an old black shawl that had shadowy blue, purple and brown plaids.

Because white flowers are tricky to hook, requiring plenty of shadows, this rug attracted a great deal of attention at the 1953 Exhibit.

Monochromatic Harmony

The use of only one color in a color plan is called a monochromatic harmony.

As you can readily see in the plate of Red, all the tints and shades of any one hue are in harmony with each other. The question is whether you want to blend them closely together, vertically, horizontally or diagonally; or use them for emphasis or accent, by skipping both values and intensities, as you might wish to do in certain geometric designs.

For example, choose any light weak from the reds for background A,

and a medium value of rather weak intensity for background B, with a good sequence of dark dull to light bright, or dark bright to light dull for the border, and you have covered the greater area of this design. Medium dark values and moderate light intensities may be used for the center detail on the light background, and very dark values of brighter intensity on the medium background. Such a monochromatic harmony is especially suited to modern décor.

To give any monochromatic harmony interest, you must have a variety of both values and intensities. Using these variations in short or long steps from one shade or tint to another, in any of the three directions, vertically, horizontally or diagonally, is bound to be harmonious.

There is no rule that you have to make your rugs in an exact monochromatic. You can create pleasing color plans which give their simple *effect*, without necessarily following hard and fast rules. In fact, you add charm to all your color plans (once you understand the underlying principles) by daring to veer off the "beaten path." Then you begin to unlock your own imaginative mind in making your color developments.

Thus far, if you have been training your eye to recognize a fairly vertical path or gradation of values — a general horizontal path of gradually strengthened intensities — and the exciting diagonal sequence of change in both values and intensities — you have already become more *selective* in what you choose to combine. Your eye immediately rules out certain colors which you *now know* are not in the proper sequence.

Added interest may be given to a monochromatic through neutrals, oftentimes in small areas of background, such as you often have in a geometric. But the use of the extreme contrast of black and white depends much on the type of design you are developing. For instance, black is, as a rule, safe for backgrounds of either floral and scroll patterns or geometric or repeat patterns, but white is pretty striking used for the same purpose. If the effect of white is necessary, it is better to use a very "dirty white"; or those gray-whites which are around the eighth value. The use of black and white in monochromatics in smaller areas will make the differences in other values sharper.

The *areas* in which you apply either your hues or neutrals in a monochromatic are discussed in another chapter. However, until you reach it, generally speaking, the most pleasing effects are achieved when you use a great quantity of the low or middle values of weak or moderate intensity, with smaller areas of the higher values and stronger intensities.

Thus, in choosing your materials, seek those hues which are soft and subdued for the greater area of a design (which is often background), and those of stronger intensity for accent and emphasis. Watch your values to get contrast, using some light, some dark, and also watch your intensities, using some weak and some bright, to give it snap and "oomph." If it is to be a dramatic development, scrimp on or skip the medium values.

A more practical way of realizing how many tints and shades of one color you have to choose from is to refer to the list of dyes given you. You will note, for instance, that you have eleven dyes to choose from in the reds alone. Using any of these dyes to get both weak and strong intensities in both dark and light values would give you a limitless amount of color with which to work.

You can still have the simplicity and feeling of a monochromatic if you pep up certain small areas of the detail of a design with highlights or shadows of a neighboring hue.

In a monochromatic, or one nearly so, let one value dominate over the others, using it again and again in developing the detail (sometimes possibly even as background), or to give the feeling that this particular value covers a greater area than the others.

In dyeing for such simple color harmonies, it is often easier to have a gradation of values to dye over, instead of just white material. For instance, a series of dark to light grays (being neutral) may be used for any hue, with white for the lightest values. They may be dyed in the manner necessary to follow the path of your choice, the vertical path being the easiest.

You can secure a fairly good horizontal path by dyeing over only one value of gray (depending upon which level you are traveling), increasing the strength of dye each step. You may have to dye over white to get the strongest intensity.

In the diagonal path, you would use the gradations of grays for the lower values, but because each step up in value becomes more intense, as well as lighter, you would probably have to dye over white somewhere around the middle to the lighter values. You might also sometimes have to add another dye to the original one, to get the increasing intensity you desire.

It is fun, too, to experiment with what you can get over gradations of other colors, and use them for monochromatics, such as:

Over browns, tans, cream and white try Cardinal, Maroon, Mahogany, Terra Cotta or Coral.

Over a gradation of golds, yellows, cream and white try Coral, Salmon, Peach, Apricot, Rust, Mummy Brown, Ecru, Khaki Drab or Bronze.

Over a gradation of dull grayed blues, medium to light blue and white, try Myrtle Green, Reseda Green, Turquoise Green, Jade, Peacock, Copenhagen Blue, Royal Blue, Navy, Bright Purple or Violet. "Over-dyeing" will produce some beautiful "off-shades."

Many greens may be used "as is." You can grade them, just as they are, in interesting changes of value and intensity, so it is seldom necessary to dye over them, except bright Kelley Green which I would spot with darker greens, or strip the color from it.

Since purples and lavenders are scarce, I hoard them and seldom use them for such over-dyeing.

So our hooked rugs are really a law unto themselves. We

must not lose our own imagination and creativeness in being GUIDED by fundamentals. Imagination, when well directed, is the most important feature in developing beautiful rugs.

Go back to theory when you lose your way, but it is only when you wing your way upon "the magic carpet of imagination" that you *really* get the greatest joy from this craft.

I can now hear you say: "But you cannot apply monotone harmony to a floral and scroll or border design." Oh yes you can! Just look at the colored sketch on the cover of my book "YOU . . . Can Hook Rugs." If the leaves had been developed of any of the weaker intensities in the first or second vertical rows on page 292, and the shadows of the fuchsias had been a pinkish-gray instead of a bluish-gray, it would be a monochromatic of reds, the black background being a neutral. Such a color harmony might well fit into modern decoration.

Now let's plan theoretically a monochromatic, as applied to #20B, "Wild Rose Lattice," herein. The outer background might be a very dark Reseda Green, the inner background a tint of it, lined off with an extremely grayed medium value of the Reseda Green, the latter repeated in the diamond background under the center flower. All the roses might be varied values of white, with shadows of grays and grayed-greens where the petals curl over. The centers of the wild roses might be a small black and white check, dyed in Turquoise Green. The leaves might be a variety of values and intensities of Reseda Green, and Myrtle Green with emphasized highlights of Aqua Green, especially where the leaves lie against the outer dark background.

But if you add imagination to your plan, you might use a purplish-gray shadow, and make the centers and stamens of the wild roses (which cover a very small area) of Chartreuse or Old Gold, and hook little caps of Mulberry and Orchid. You would then give it much more interest, yet still maintain its simplicity of coloring.

[62]

Of the rugs which you may see at Rose Cottage, there is a lovely "Craighead" made by Ruth Van Ornum of Los Angeles, Calif., Teacher, in which a very dark background of navy makes a dramatic contrast to its white roses which are shadowed in very light grays and grayed blues. Other flowers of delicate grays have shadowy detail or centers of medium gray and grayed-blues, and the grapes of grayish blues have white highlights. Imagination has been added, without losing the effect of a monochromatic plan, by making the foliage of a taupy-gray (which is really a complement), yet it is so near the neutral pole that you are not conscious of but one hue, blue.

WHEN YOU study "Queen's Desire," hooked by Mrs. Gloria Rindge of Ware, Mass., Mrs. Gladys Skiffington, Teacher, first visualize the lovely room for which it was made. It is a fireplace rug on a gray broadloom carpet, with a pair of red fireside chairs on either side. The walls are a pinky-red with draperies of gray satin with a tiny Chinese figure of red. The red bowls of lamps are set on black onyx bases with white lamp shades. Now think of the entire rug as having a gray feeling, the outer background being black, the middle area between the scrolls and ribbon a medium gray, and the inner background very light gray.

Neutral scrolls of varied grays, from very dark accenting shadows of novelty weaves and textures, blending gradually lighter into accented curls of chalky white, were all veined with varied reds (Cardinal and Egyptian Red over tweedy mixture), using the darker values for the center veins and the lighter values for lateral veins.

The center rose which was the "star" in this color plan was a bright rich red and blended from dark shadows (weak Navy over red) into natural brighter reds, while the other roses were of lighter values and somewhat duller intensities of varied reds.

The general effect of the hibiscus was a mahogany-red with darker values of rich Maroon at center.

The lilies and carnations were both delicate, the former of varied Old Golds with accents of darker Mummy Brown and tints of Bronze Green for the throats, while the petals of the latter were white at the base, blending into tints of Aqualon Yellows with Old Gold shadows. Their raggedy edges were accented with spot-dyed Cherry and Gold.

The parrot tulips and phlox were extremely soft Violet, but tints of red, such as pale Aqualon Pink blended back into the darker Violet and blues, with a few very dark accents of deep RP and P. Each petal of the phlox was hooked either of blue or violet to make one stand out against another, and they all had centers of black and white checks tinted with green.

Gray to white pussy willows and extremely grayed blue-green tulip leaves and grayed yellow-green rose leaves added to the neutrality of this rug, and gave it a monochromatic feeling.

The ribbon was developed in a two-sided manner, so that as it turned, it was white on one side (Silver Gray to beige to dirty white to white), and the varied reds of the rose on the other side.

Most teachers have their own local Exhibits each year, and Gladys Skiffington's are always an attraction because of her artistry with color.

TWIN SCOTTIES

THREE ROSE OVAL

THE MATERIALS used in "Twin Scotties," hooked by Mrs. R. W. White of Detroit, Mich., Teacher, were natural, "as is," no dyeing being necessary. The general coloring was a range of seven or eight values, from very light cream to dark brown. The inner background was warm golden tan, a nubby blanket that added texture to the rug.

A brown plaid skirt, with flashes of Terra Cotta, was combined with medium and light plain brown materials for the jagged border, softening and lightening as they met the lighter inner background.

The dogs were shaded of lighter values and of a more grayed tone. Additional contour was given to the dogs which where changed to Sealyhams by the directional line of hooking to form the curve of the body. Dark brown shadowed the eyes, nose and mouth. A bit of Terra Cotta from the plaid skirt and a faded grayed rose material seemed just right to give the tongue a realistic look, and a lovely soft blue formed the roguish eyes.

Thus, this kiddie's rug for Ricky, her grandson, not only brings delight to a youngster, but adds a lot to a pine-paneled room covered with a dark brown and green textured carpet, with draperies of the warm golden tan of the inner background.

DISCRIMINATION was shown in the choice of "Three Rose Oval," hooked by Mrs. Robert Bussom of Shelby, Ohio, Mrs. Frank Hruby, Teacher, for a century old house furnished with treasured antiques. Dove gray woodwork and a gray and white patterned wallpaper provided the keynote for the color plan.

A collection of very old gray materials was used for most of the rug. Dark gray was used under the flowered center, and a medium gray tweed for the remainder of the inner background, with old black outside the scroll.

Some of the varied gray materials were put through an extremely grayed solution of Aqua-Green dye, to turn it only the slightest bit from pure gray. Some of it was spot-dyed with extremely weak Maroon and weak Aqua Green. These were applied to the scroll, which was first veined with red plaid materials, softened with a little Aqua Green dye. The dark values of the spot-dyed grays were used next to the vein on the outside of the scroll, and shaded into light gray edges, which met the black outside background. On the other side of the vein, the lighter values of the spot-dyed grays were shaded into dark gray edges where they met the light gray inside background.

The roses were of gay and bright reds, which had been put through varied baths of Maroon dye. In its darker values, the rose blended into blackish reds; in its lighter values, small amounts of the real bright reds were used for highlights. The foliage was developed of the gray materials which had been given a little more of the intensity of the Aqua Green dye.

In its final effect, the color plan has a feeling of a monochromatic harmony of reds and gray, because the foliage is such a greenish gray.

JEFFERSON DAVIS

ALL THE floral detail in "Jefferson Davis," hooked by Mrs. John L. Reese of Pensacola, Fla., Mrs. Albert J. Giacomini, Teacher, has the effect of being one hue, yet there is considerable individuality in the development of the three different types of flowers. The intensity (equal parts of Terra Cotta and American Beauty) has been applied to the gloxinia-like blossoms, with deep, rich throat and edges, flushing out to delicate tints where the petals roll over. These same hues have been carried forward into the veins of the scrolly blue-green leaves (equal parts of Reseda and Green).

The large roses are an extremely grayed pink (equal parts of Mahogany and Terra Cotta), and flush out to almost white edges. Their hues have been carried forward into the veins of the rose leaves of yellow-greens (Bronze Green).

The third and less important bell-like flower is a bronzy-white (Bronze over white), repeating the same blue-greens in the leaves, veined with Bronze.

The detail which catches and holds the eye is the delicate manner in which all the tints of blue-green, yellow-green and bronze have been blended into the ferny detail, with many of the tips turning to pinkish-white, thus reflecting the floral hue.

The extra dark blackish-brown all-over background (one part Black, two parts Dark Brown) brings out with dramatic clarity all of the floral detail.

This design was inspired by an old needlepoint rug, which is now in the Jefferson Davis Museum in Montgomery, Ala.

Adjacent or Analogous Harmony

Before starting any new chapter, do go back and re-read the previous chapters. We sometimes do not get the FULL sense of theory until we re-read it in the light of later knowledge and experience. As we re-read, reiteration gives the old a *new* meaning. It also gets you "in the groove" and gives continuity to this subject.

Any two hues which adjoin each other are harmonious because they are related through a common basic color element, and will "flow together" because of their close proximity. Glance at the Color Tree and notice how any two just naturally blend together.

Let's trace this relationship down:

P blends with RP because both are made up partly from Red
RP	"	"	R	"	RP	is	"	"	"	"	"
R	"	"	YR	"	YR	"	"	"	"	"	"
YR	"	"	Y	"	YR	"	"	"	"	"	Yellow
Y	"	"	GY	"	GY	"	"	"	"	"	"
GY	"	"	G	"	both are	"	"	"	"	"
G	"	"	BG	"	"	"	"	"	"	"	Blue
BG	"	"	B	"	BG	is	"	"	"	"	"
B	"	"	PB	"	PB	"	"	"	"	"	"
PB	"	"	P	"	both are	"	"	"	"	"

Notice as you glance down the extreme right side above that all of these colors stem from Red, Yellow and Blue.

The vertical, horizontal and diagonal paths referred to in monochromatic harmonies now also take on both a lateral and spiral movement as they extend in these three directions.

The upward path in values must now necessarily become lateral as it climbs. Thus, in the vertical path you step over into the second hue at any point of value, combining the vertical with the lateral path. For example, starting with a very dark value of Red-purple and ascending vertically to the middle value; then stepping over into R, continuing to climb in the R to the top.

RP									v		R						
				8	6	4	2	1	8	1	2	4	6				
			10	8	6	4	2	1	7	1	2	4	6	8			
16	14	12	10	8	6	4	2	1	6	1	2	4	6	8	10	12	
16	14	12	10	8	6	4	2	1	5	1	2	4	6	8	10	12	14
		12	10	8	6	4	2	1	4	1	2	4	6	8	10	12	14
			10	8	6	4	2	1	3	1	2	4	6	8	10		

You have probably already done this in shading a rose from rich Strawberry (dye) shadows to highlights from a tint of Maroon. In shading a dark green leaf to a light yellow-green tip, you have proven how easy it is to step over from G into its neighbor YG.

Likewise the horizontal path, instead of extending straight out from a weak to a strong intensity of one hue (same values), now also has a lateral movement as it extends over into the next hue of the same value.

v	R			YR		
8						
7						
6	1	2	4	4	6	8
5						
4						
3						

Thus, the shell border detail on page 51 might shade from a grayed R, like R 4/1, R 4/2, R 4/6 into R–YR of the same value and intensity (such as a soft Rust), thence blending into an even stronger intensity of the second hue (R–YR), such as what you might refer to as Mummy Brown.

But this lateral path also may become a spiral, as it turns in a diagonal direction, especially when combining more than two hues. Thus, as you climb in value and increase in intensity (extending outward) you change from a dark grayed shade of one hue, gradually climbing upward and ever growing stronger into a light bright tint of a neighboring hue.

Practically speaking, this would be like a blend from a dark reddish brown to a medium bright Mahogany, to a light bright Peach. You would go about getting this transition, which swings from a dark dull of one hue over into a light bright of another hue, by dyeing Dark Brown in the three darkest graduating values, and Mahogany in two medium values of medium intensity, and Peach in two lighter bright values.

In using any two adjacent hues, you will find they are more harmonious and blend better when values are similar or the same, and intensities are weak or moderate, like a medium grayed plum and a medium grayed blue. As the intensities grow stronger, like a bright purple and a bright blue, the combination becomes more striking. You might use the former in floral or leaf detail, but a line or two of brighter intensities of two hues might be just right to lend brilliance and sparkle in the detail of a geometric or oriental design.

When analogous hues are *widely different* in *values and intensities,* especially in the brighter intensities, like a dark rich Royal Blue (PB–P) and a light, bright Peacock (BG–B), they are often too dramatic to blend when hooked. Because of their difference in both value and intensity, each holds its own character. This might sometimes work out to good advantage, giving richness to the colors in certain geometric or Oriental detail. A single line of one of them gives a dashing accent.

Any hue appears less intense if you hook a neutral or an extremely grayed shade of the hue (and of about the same value) next to it, such as a slightly purplish-gray to pull down the intensity of a bright purple.

The use of only TWO adjacent hues is VERY CLOSE harmony.

Now, of MORE interest are THREE or more adjacent hues BETWEEN TWO PRIMARIES, or those adjacent hues which include but ONE primary. Thus, you could include all colors BETWEEN Red and Yellow — Yellow and Blue — and Blue and Red.

Or, you can include ONE primary and swing to one or both sides of it, but not far enough to include another primary. As an example, BG, B (primary), PB and P.

Analogous harmonies have an emotional quality, too, in that you may "warm them up" or "cool them down" by swinging as far as you wish toward the warm or the cool side.

Thus, an analogous harmony could include B, BG, G, and be warmed up by GY, or go the other way, B, PB, P, RP, and be warmed with very little of RP–R. A warm combination of Y, GY and G could be cooled by BG.

Or, one part of the design may be in an analogous harmony which could be on the warm side, like Y, GY, G, and be cooled off in a floral center by adding the opposite color, like PB or P. But more on this phase later.

Don't forget your neutrals or hues of such grayness that they appear almost gray, in planning these harmonies. Use them as a break — a place for the eye to rest. You have a wide choice.

The color paths for three or more hues are the same as those for two hues.

Put your varied materials of any adjoining hues together now, and visualize how they might be used to develop a scroll. For instance, choose a dark, dull shadow from one hue, with gradually lighter and brighter hues of its neighbors to form an interesting diagonal color path. Confine the bright intensities to small areas, tips or edges, and use the intermediate shades of medium intensity and value, for the greater area.

In handling your materials, you will find yourself weeding out those which are too harsh or too weak, or which do not please you. This ability of SELECTION of materials is good practice for you, and will develop your sense of color.

As you look at a black and white illustration, let your imaginative mind see it in harmonious combinations of analogous hues of your own choice — not just one group, but several groups.

Look now at any scroll illustrated herein and visualize it from dark Plum to medium Burgundy into tints of Wine (P–RP and RP). Now think of it again as shading from a dark dull Royal Blue to medium Purple and light Orchid (PB–P, P and P–RP). Now think of it shading from dark Reseda Green to medium Turquoise Green and light Aqua (G, G–BG and B). Or can you visualize it shading from dark Seal Brown, medium Golden Brown to Champagne and tints of Old Gold (YR and YR–Y)? These are only a few. You dream up some of your own!

But to help you visualize an analogous harmony, suppose we apply one of YR, Y, GY, G to #503, "Seven Sisters," illustrated herein.

Since the scroll is dominating, and plays the leading part in the design, we might use YR, applying it in many values and intensities of browns to cream, as its most dominant color, playing it down against a Seal Brown outer background and an Old Ivory inner background.

In the floral center, a lovely rich Rust rose will provide the intensity of this color, but it will blend into highlights of soft yellow, and these two will be repeated in one of the pansies. As a contrast in values, the lily will be creamy white, with varied rusty freckles. Creamy white will be repeated in the three lower petals of the other pansy, with gold whiskers and velvety Seal Brown upper petals. Differences in two flowers of a kind are a surprise and a delight to the eye. The dahlia will be a Golden Brown with Ecru highlights. A light, soft Yellow wild rose is shadowed with brown and highlighted with cream. Creamy white forms the throat of the morning glory, and blends into light Golden Brown edges. The tulip will be a very grayed Nugget Gold, with accents at base of Rust and edges of Bronze.

Dark Seal Brown, dull, dark Olive Green and Dark Green will fill the background spaces around the center flowers, and shadow the base of all the leaves that disappear under the center flowers. The rose leaves or other broad leaves will blend in a vertical gradation of GY (Bronze Green dye), and long tulip leaves or smaller ones will be in a similar gradation from Green dye.

Thus, I have given it what all good color plans need, *interest* by variety and contrast of values and intensities, *unity* by small areas of strong intensity and larger areas of moderate or weak intensity, and *repetition* by repeating the hues over and over again. One hue, YR, dominates.

Yet, as in all color plans, this is only a skeleton description. Most ruggers know that as one hooks, small changes have to be made, to strengthen or tie the detail more closely together. However, a discussion of a definite color plan helps to visualize the possibilities of other colors, and with the knowledge you accumulate, you can use other color plans of *your* choice and go ahead with a fair degree of certainty that you can't be too far wrong in the final result.

Season's Promise (a pair)

A MODERN room of a beloved son is graced by this "Season's Promise," hooked by Mrs. Florence Ordway of Jackson, Michigan, Teacher. Light gray carpets with charcoal walls, coffeetable of black, and wrought iron lamps with white shades are accented by a bright red davenport. Draperies combining the red, grays and white complete the setting.

The rug, used before the davenport, repeats its gay reds in the tulips (Scarlet dye over varied whites and grays, with Terra Cotta added for deepest shades). The pussy willows are of varied grays. The foliage repeats the greens of the draperies, using Bronze Green, Reseda and Bronze dyes. Delicate tints of the red from the tulips and greens from the foliage were spotted over varied neutral grays for the scrolls, which shaded from darker values at center sides to lighter values at outer edges and at ends.

The inner background is cream (an old blanket), shadowed under the tulips by gradation dyeing of Old Ivory, plus a bit of Bronze. The outer background is black.

AN ANALOGOUS color harmony of PB, P and RP was used in "Season's Promise," hooked by Marjorie Humphries of Meriden, Connecticut, Teacher. The outer background of navy blue is not too much of a contrast to the inner background of slate blue.

The dominating hue is RP, and in its intensity is applied to the tulips in seven values of this formula, dyed over varied whites: 1 teaspoon Mulberry, 1/4 teaspoon Violet and 1/16 teaspoon Rust. The veins of its petals are deep, rich purples, flanked by purple material spot-dyed with the tulip formula, so that the latter is somewhat grayed and produces a dull mauve. The stamens are black and the pistils old gold. Notice how the varied values have been hooked in a directional line to give additional flare to the petals. The dark shadows give additional depth between the front and rear petals.

The pussy willows are gray and white check "as is" with caps of medium tan checks, delicately spot-dyed with leaf formula.

The leaves, of a dark, dull YG (1 teaspoon Bright Green, 1/4 teaspoon Bronze Green and 1/32 teaspoon Buttercup Yellow), are broadly veined with very dark values, and sink somewhat into the background. Only an occasional line of light bluish-gray (weak Reseda and Turquoise Green over a grayed tweed) has been used in the turnover of the leaves.

The veins of the scroll were hooked in dull purples, spot-dyed with the tulip formula; flanked by a medium dark gray on one side, and by a gray and white check on the other. The edge of the scroll was accented with creamy white, blending into three or four lines of the tints for tulips before using pale gray, spot-dyed with the tulip formula, for the remainder. Following the contour of the veins gave it rhythm.

WHIPPLE

"WHIPPLE" was hooked by Mrs. Alma Newton of Sidney, N. Y., Mrs. O. H. Collett, Teacher. Mrs. Collett has graciously given you the formulas for the development of this beautiful geometric, as follows:

#1, *all dyed over white materials:*
    A, two light values of Buttercup Yellow.
    B, several medium values of four parts Buttercup Yellow, one part Apricot and one part Mummy Brown.
    C, several darker values of B, to which more Mummy Brown is added each time, so there are eleven shades of #1 in all.

#2, *all dyed over white materials:*
    A, two light values from equal parts of Mummy Brown and Medium Brown.
    B, gradually darken A with Mummy Brown to secure three more values of #2.

#3, *all over white and brown materials:*
    A, equal parts of Mummy Brown and Medium Brown for light values.
    B, gradually darken A and dye over brown materials with more Mummy Brown each time, the darkest to be a very dark brown to get eight values in all of #3.

#4, *Bronze Green over odd grays,* for three values of very grayed greens.

The background is of the dark browns of #3 formula, using the very darkest value around the rosettes. The border is edged with dark of #3 and filled with dark of #2, except the little wiggles of the soft golds from #1.

The conventional motif is outlined with a warm brownish-tan from formula #1 and its outer area filled with shades from #2. Its center cross-like motif is outlined with a couple of lines of rather bright gold in about a medium value, from formula #1, and is filled with a very light yellowish-cream, the lightest of #1. As an additional individual touch, a little dark accent of the darkest of #3 was used where the cross-like motif pinches inward.

The gold rosettes vary, some are a little brighter than others. The petals are shaded with #1 group, with shadows at the base of the lightest of #3. Its center has outlines of the darkest gold of #1, and one from #3, and is filled with the light to dark of #4, which is a very grayed Bronze Green.

Gale Oval

Harmony

SOMETIMES the choice of the right design calls for an oval. Very dark Seal Brown is used for the outer background of "Gale Oval" hooked by Mrs. Paul Wood of Braintree, Mass., Bertha Brousseau, Teacher. Its inner background is a warm, slightly "goldish" brown, a subtle change in value. The scrolls were of browns, spot-dyed with gold, green and mahogany. Their edges and the curling ends are highlighted with a very delicate shade of pinkish-mahogany, a reflection from the two roses in the center. Their veins are a deep reddish mahogany.

The roses of rich rusty mahogany have highlights falling upon only one side of each of the roses. They shade down to very dark brownish shadows. The phlox between them is extremely grayed, of a medley of blues and lavenders with white centers and a little blackish spot in the center of each blossom. The small five-petaled padulas at the end of the bouquet are in varied greenish-blues. The rose hips at the end repeat the colors of the roses, as do the other little buds around the floral center.

The leaf foliage is a lovely blue-green. Considerable shadow accent is used in those which disappear under the center flowers. The highlights have been fingered well back from the tips of some of those that overlie others. They are all veined with the rusty mahogany shades of the roses.

"HARMONY," hooked by Mrs. Velma Bradbury, Syracuse, N. Y., Lydia Hicks, Teacher, has a background of Navy over gray. Its scroll is of neutral grays, veined with the brightest of the morning glories, a rich RP (American Beauty dye). Some of the RP glories are less intense (Wild Rose dye), blending into pinky whites, while others are in soft analogous hues of PB (Plum), and B–BGs (Peacock). Imagination is shown in the way off-white has been carried from the scroll into the light throats of the morning glories, and into the edges of the leaves.

The foliage has been played down through extra dark and a very weak BG or GY near the midribs, turning to edges of the neutral grays from the scroll in the outer area of the bouquet. Their veins are varied, being repetitions from all the morning glories. The buds are dark to light values of adjacent flowers.

Complementary Harmony

Any two exact opposites are called complementary. Each is the most perfect contrast for the other. Each makes the other LOOK brighter.

We see Nature's examples of it in blue and purple flowers, with YR and GY centers.

Thus, so far as the major hues are concerned, your complementary contrasts are:

Red and Blue-Green ⎫ These three are often
Yellow and Purple-Blue ⎬ more striking than the
Blue and Yellow-Red ⎭ others.
Green and Red-Purple
Purple and Green-Yellow

You will also note that in all but Green and Red-Purple, one is a cool color and the other a warm, and this takes care of that phase of balance.

Complementary harmonies have two color paths, one horizontal, and the other diagonal and oblique, which brings the two opposites together.

If the path be horizontal, you go straight from one hue into its opposite, through the Neutral Pole, like this:

R		v		BG
		8		
		7		
		6		
6 4 2 1		5	1 2 4 6	
		4		
		3		

Such a blend would probably only be used in certain geometric or Oriental details. For example, a medium mahogany motif that grows grayer toward its edge, and then has an accenting outline of a very grayed BG, and one a little brighter (but all of the same value). Since it is a horizontal path, the effect would be flat, having no shadow or highlight. In such a path, one hue should be used in excess of the other.

The path may be diagonal through the two which will bring them together in harmony.

BG					v	R						
	4	2	1		8	1 2 4 6						
	6	4	2	1	7	1 2-4 6 8						
8	6	4	2	1	6	1/2 4 6 8 10 12						
	6	4	2/1		5	1 2 4 6 8 10 12 14						
	6	4/2	1		4	1 2 4 6 8 10 12 14						
	6/4	2	1		3	1 2 4 6 8 10						

The above diagram will help you visualize a scroll blending from a very dark, moderately bright BG, gradually shading lighter and grayer, into a medium light greenish-gray; then matching its value and intensity, changing to a medium light reddish-gray (like R 6/1, see plate of Red), and thence into grayish-pink, with possibly small accents of a lighter and slightly brighter pink (like R 7/2).

You will note that in combining BG with red, I crossed through the Neutral Pole at BG 6/1 into R 6/1, which brings the two complements together where their differences are the slightest. Thus, when blending from one hue to its opposite, as you might in a scroll, use the *same weak intensity* of the *same value* in *both* hues, where they meet. You can't bring two complementaries together smoothly in their full intensities. Thus, if you desire to accentuate them, as you might do in a geometric or an Oriental, by all means use similar intensities of both hues. For instance, a bright Coral and a light Jade of strong intensities would be too dramatic for use in the detail of most hooked rugs, though they might be used to accent certain small detail in geometrics or Orientals.

But, practically speaking, as applied to hooked rugs, you can also use the vertical or diagonal path in each separate color, such as you might do in blending a flower in a diagonal path of one hue, or a leaf in a vertical path in its opposite.

[83]

If a bright red rose is hooked against a bright blue-green leaf, the complementary of each adds something to the other. The effect is more powerful when complementary colors are of equal intensity. If unequal, the most saturated or brightest intensity will gain strength — the weak or grayed one will appear even weaker.

If values are far apart (like very dark and very light), any two weak intensities of complementaries appear brighter when used together, than when used alone. For instance, a very dark and very grayed BG and a very light R, like a tint of Mahogany over white, would both appear extremely grayed, when viewed separately, but placed together, as you might for a dark outer background and a light inner background, both take on added intensity.

If you want a soft and subtle effect, limit yourself to very little of strong intensity in *one* of the two complements, and keep all others weak or moderate. For instance, a small amount of light Jade, as the accent at edge of a BG scroll which shades from medium light BG to darker and duller BG, offsets a larger quantity of a dull reddish Mahogany used for exaggerated veins. Thus, the intensity appears only in the BG.

The lower you go in the scale of values (darker), and the nearer to the Neutral Pole (weak intensity), the more freely you can use complementary harmony without harshness.

Now you do not have to stick to strict theory in making hooked rugs, but just as following good principles in daily living keeps you out of trouble, so does following the principles of color harmony.

When the contrasts of complementaries are brought together in proper subdued hues, they create a glowing brilliance and richness that give charm to this type of harmony, but it is only when you combine the *proper* values and intensities that you cause one to enhance the other. Therefore, choose those intensities which complement or soften the others, as the

[84]

case may be. Let one be the "star," and the other play the "supporting lead."

Remember, too, the problem of the afterimage, for it must always be reckoned with in complementaries. All surrounding detail or background near a brilliant color will be somewhat affected by the influence of the afterimage. Thus, a brilliant red flower may cause a blue flower near by to take on a greenish cast, because the complement of red is blue-green.

In dyeing, it is easy to bring two complements together, by putting each one into a weak solution of its opposite. Harmonizing them is also done in two other ways, one by spot-dyeing a gray of the right value (where you intend to change from one hue to another) with weak dye of both colors, and use it as a transition from one hue into the other. The other way is to follow my progressive dyeing, by dipping one end of a gray of the right value into a very weak solution of one dye, and the other end in a very weak solution of the complementary dye, permitting them to run together at the center where each will gray the other down. Then you have in one piece of material an easy transition from one hue to the other.

Of course, dyeing any *colored* material with the dye of its complement will gray it down toward the neutral pole. Thus, Turkey Red and Kelley Green, two of the most plentiful materials to ruggers, may be turned to gorgeous flower and leaf tones by dyeing any of the blue-green dyes, such as Reseda or Green, or even Peacock (but go easy on the latter because of its intensity) in various strengths over the Turkey Red material for flowers. Also dye any of the red dyes over the Kelley Green material in different strengths of dye for leaf detail.

In your hooked rug, much depends upon *how* you combine your complementaries in their various values and intensities, for it is the *proportion* of each that decides whether you have given it contrast and interest, or made your whole color scheme appear harsh and vibrant, one hue vying with the other. But more about proportion and areas in a later chapter. Did you see "The Robe" in technicolor? Didn't you love the beautiful mahogany and blue complementary contrasts of that picture?

Generally, the larger the quantity and the greater the area to which it is applied, the brighter complementaries will appear. Contrariwise, very small amounts of each used in any all-over design will merge and weaken the intensities of both (as viewed from a distance), and make them appear as gray. At a fashion show, I admired the "gray checked dress" of a model, only to find, when she appeared close at hand, that the design was made of little squares closely spaced, of complementary blue and mahogany. At another time I admired the "gray tailored suit" worn by one of my teachers, only to discover it was really a very fine diagonal weave of green and red.

Really, color sense depends so much upon the individual, and how he applies his knowledge. You must make the effort to train your eye to become analytical and selective. It is only when you exercise this power that you are conscious of it, and it is only as you continue to use this power that you eliminate the possibility of losing it.

If you have thoroughly absorbed the principles of color harmony, you will still find yourself automatically following rules to a great extent, by your *choice* and *selection* of color, but not to the point of stifling imagination.

Now let's consider a complementary harmony in this light, as applied to #567, "Filigree," herein, using a combination of RP and G. The background might be one of the Gs, in a medium dark, dull value, such as you might get from Myrtle Green. The little leafy border of the hexagon might be veined with a medium light G, and filled with a light and somewhat grayed RP, possibly from Mulberry. The area of background within this border might be a richer and darker value of Myrtle Green, and the area of background around the fingered motif might be a light greenish gray. The little border that separates these two background areas might be a combination of your varied values of Myrtle Green and Mulberry. The fingered motif of deep, rich Mulberry might be darker at its center (around its "islands"), shading out to slightly lighter values at the tips of the fingers. The "fingers" might be outlined in a light, bright green, possibly Aqua Green. Now the little islands at the center of this motif may be of three different values of G, edged with contrasting values of RP.

The intervening figures between the hexagons might be of a light value of RP, shading it back into very dark values around the center and edged with light bright G. G may be used for accents at the center, again contrasting the values and intensities where the two hues meet. Thus, G has been used to a greater degree, yet both colors have wide variance of values and intensities, some being light, some weak, some dull and some bright, the ingredients of an interesting color plan.

REED OVAL

SINCE a rather gay red is used in various values and intensities for all the floral detail of "Reed Oval" (with braided border increasing it to 7' × 9') hooked by Mrs. Helen Spencer of Palmer, Mass., Harriet Snow, Teacher, its complement of BG was used in soft and gray intensities.

The first two braids carried out the general taupy shade (Taupe spot-dyed over light tan) of the background of the hooked rug, which extends beyond the dark oval border. Then they began to weave into the light, soft grayed greens of the foliage. As they extend outward, they grow gradually darker and a bit more intense, and then turn duller and weave into dark taupe. From a taupe they turn into a very dark and dull grayed red, gradually growing brighter and lighter, reflecting the reds from the flowered center. The red braids then grow gradually darker and duller, and turn to black at the edge of the rug, like the background of the oval band.

The colors of this rug were taken from a handmade quilt on an antique maple bed in the room where the rug was to be used. All the dyeing for the hooking and braiding was done at the same time.

The reds were developed in seven values from this formula: two parts Cardinal, one part Magenta, one part Maroon over light neutrals. They were used for all the floral detail, including the buds in the narrow border. One of the roses blended from extremely dark, grayed reds up to rather gay, bright red accents, while the other two had very little highlight, and were predominantly darker than the first one. All the other flowers were in other varied values of red — some being quite light.

The greens were dyed in five values from this formula: equal parts of Myrtle Green and Reseda Green over yellow. They were used for all the foliage in the background of the hooked rug which extends beyond the dark oval border. Their stems were of the same dyed material, spot-dyed with the reds, which made them of somewhat dark values and dull intensities.

OAK LEAVES

A LEAF design is an easy rug to live with, especially when its colors are very muted.

The outside background of #8A, "Oak Leaves," hooked by Mrs. Sally W. Pollitt of Pascagoula, Miss., Alice J. Otis, Teacher, was a dark Plum secured from Turkey Red over navy blue trousers gathered from friends and family. The inside background was a grayish-tan blanket.

The square lines marking off each block were of the plum outer background, flanked with green and rose-tan plaids from an old coat. This plaid also appeared as the short straight lines in the outside border.

Each block of four leaves was hooked in a vertical gradation of values of two complementary colors, R and BG. One block was of soft grayed rose hues (Crimson and Terra Cotta) with green veins, and the alternating block was of a gradation of grayed greens (Myrtle Green and Reseda) with rose veins.

As a matter of interest, most of the materials that went into both sets of leaves were leftovers from previous rugs.

Mrs. Otis, who made her first rug under Elizabeth Spalding, Teacher, of Beloit, Wis., started her own classes in the Pascagoula Arts and Crafts Club during the war, as a means of occupying the idle time of traveling Army wives. She takes her pupils first to the kitchen. There they discuss their whole color plan and do all their dyeing, which is keyed toward overtones, or the mingling of colors to bring all together in harmony. All the dyeing is completed before they start to hook. Thus, they know before they pull the first loop through that the application of the colors of their choice will produce harmony, because the mingling of color has already taken place in the dyepot.

CHILCOTT RUNNER

"CHILCOTT RUNNER," hooked by Leona Lincoln of Weymouth, Mass., Teacher, is one of three rugs, of similar coloring, made for Sister May, to be used in her bedroom. You will note that the design is somewhat conventionalized.

The colors used in this rug were a reflection of the lovely blue-green draperies which I had brought to her from Bermuda, and a very delicate mahogany-pink upholstered chair. Only the two dyes of Mahogany and Reseda were used, but in many values. A most delicate tint of mahogany over white filled the center background, and a slightly stronger mahogany in the area of background around it. The background under the bands of the border is a deep rich Reseda.

All the flowers were well blended in a diagonal path, from a dark bright to a light dull Mahogany tint, with Reseda centers. Their buds were of darker Mahogany. All the foliage was dark Reseda on one side of the vein and light on the other side. The veins through the center and on one side of the leaves only, were of Mahogany. The delicate conventionalized stem detail in the center, so typical of the older rugs, was medium dark Reseda.

The bands which formed three different border lines were in gradations, each one shading from dark inside to light outer edge of Mahogany.

There is a good balance of dark and light values in this development, and it has been hooked in such a manner as to keep the old-fashioned effect.

HEARTS AND FLOWERS

THE BACKGROUNDS of "Hearts and Flowers," hooked by Mrs. Paul L. Willson of Saco, Maine, Mrs. Mary MacKay, Teacher, have a very close relationship. The outside is a medium dark gray, the intermediate a medium soft gray, and the inner background a light gray.

The large scroll which forms the outer border is developed of varied greens (Olive Green), veined in both Mulberry and Plum of varied values and intensities. It is darkest at the beginning, or where the curls break off from the main part and extend into extremely light tips. Many of the curling knobs blend from delicate greens into delicate tints of plum. The ends of the scroll are held together by an extremely grayed plum band which shades into an almost whitish highlight.

A fine feeling of relationship has been given to the design through the repetition of dull Mulberry and Plum shades in the center chrysanthemum, in the smaller scrolls around the floral bouquet, and again in the corner chrysanthemums. Tints of the same hues appear as the turned-over petals of the white magnolias, and in shadowy accents of the pink dogwood. The softer and lighter pinks have been used for the lilies, which have been freckled with Bronze. The tulips have been played down in a slightly brownish plum that shades out to copper edges. The little petunia-like blossoms are in extremely subdued Plum shades with highlights of delicate Mulberry in the curled back petals in the foreground and deep gold stamens in their centers. The fuchsias have curled back sepals of the Mulberry shades with Plum "skirts."

The leaf detail is most interesting, shadowing extremely dark where it disappears under the floral detail in the center, and extending into much lighter values at the tips. The magnolia leaves are quite bronzy, and curl over with an extremely grayed blue turnover. The tulip leaves repeat the darker values of the Olive Green from the outer scroll. The long ferny leaves are a combination of yellow-greens and coppery browns which tie them to both the magnolia leaves and the coppers in the tulips.

The smaller Mulberry scroll that surrounds the floral center shades from dark, dull Plum from the inner side of the curls to a light, bright Mulberry along the outer edges. The two curls which swing toward the center bouquet are more definitely purple. The values of the Mulberries and Plums are so close where they meet that they look as though a brush had drawn them together. The hearts are also Mulberry with highlights in their centers and the ferny fronds separating these scrolls repeat the same yellow-greens and bronzy shades of those in the center, and the little petunia-like blossoms are of the same purples and Plums with Mulberry highlights.

The corner detail repeats the same colors of the center.

This is an excellent example of the complementary harmony of RP and G.

Double Complementary Harmony

A double complementary harmony is a challenge to your imagination. It is a combination of any two sets of complements. One set should dominate over the other, the second set being used with discretion and in lower intensities. Otherwise a double complement would be developed much as a complementary.

The more neighborly they are, as in this sketch,

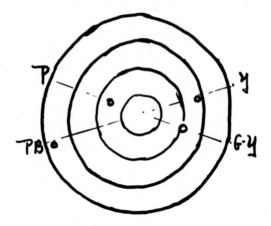

the easier they will blend. Remember that one hue should dominate. Keep in mind, too, the circle of intensities, and use only one of your hues in bright intensity. As an example, if purple blue is to be the brightest one in the above set of double complements, use its complement Y in less intensity, and the other set of two complements still less intense, as indicated by the dots on the circle of intensities.

A good example of a double complement is in the "Goddess of Fortuna," illustrated herein in color.

Split Complementaries

Each hue has two colors which are split complements combining one hue with the two hues which lie on each side of its direct opposite, as in this sketch.

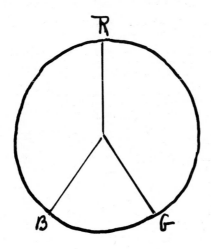

Always start with the key color, which is to *dominate*, and split on its complement. The two split complements should be subdued in comparison, though they may cover a greater area.

If any of the three colors is a primary, *start* with it, and split on its complement, but don't split a primary.

It is an interesting harmony, for two of the hues are in close relationship, while the third — or key color — introduces an entirely different and contrasting note. You will also note that if the key color is a warm one (as in the above sketch), it is balanced by either one or two cool colors and vice versa.

So, *start* your split complementaries

ON	AND SPLIT ON
Red	Blue and Green
Yellow	Purple and Blue
Green-Yellow	Purple-Blue and Red-Purple
Green	Purple and Red
Blue	Red and Yellow
Purple	Yellow and Green
Red-Purple	Green-Yellow and Blue-Green

Thus, you will notice you would never start on YR, BG or PB because you would then be splitting on B, R and Y, all primaries.

The Color Paths are the same as in complementary harmony. An excellent example of a split complementary harmony is "The Perfume Box," herein in color.

Near complements — that is, the two hues next to any two complements are called near complements.

Triad Harmony

Since Munsell divided the Color Wheel into 10 major hues instead of 12, confining what we formerly called orange (YR) to a small area, it can no longer be divided into four equal parts, to give a combination of three equally distant hues, which was the old theory of triad harmony. Because of this inequality, the points of a triad would only fall directly upon the center of one of the three hues, the other two points falling between the two hues.

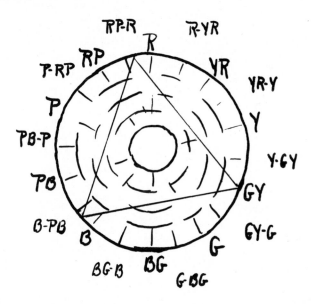

However, since the other two fall nearer one hue than another, for all practical purposes that is near enough to carry out the plan of a triad harmony as applied to our hooked rugs.

You will note that two of the colors will be warm, and the other one cool, or vice versa (unless one of the three is on the fence). Since the hues are widely separated, use this harmony with extreme care, especially in applying the colors to its varied areas. Develop the largest area of the weakest hue; the smaller ones of the strongest color; and the intermediate areas of the third color in moderate intensity.

Now the Color Paths take a swirling or circular path through the Color Sphere.

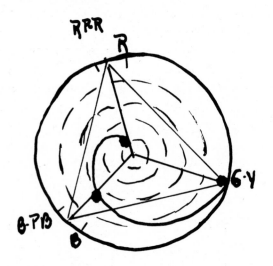

One may be horizontal (all in the same value). Visualize its path as it passes through the sphere, because it not only travels two thirds the way around the wheel, but also travels inward toward the grayer shades. Thus, a moderately bright YG (in any one of the eight values) may gradually turn grayer into a more moderate intensity of the *same value* of B, which will also grow grayer into a very, very grayed R of the same value, which you might refer to as a "warm gray."

But the diagonal path is much more interesting. It also swings upward, as well as inward. For instance, a dark, bright YG may gradually grow lighter and a bit duller into a B of more moderate intensity, but a bit lighter, and thence into a very, very light warm gray, like R 8/1. Thus, as the path strikes inward, and also moves upward, it lightens the value as it decreases the intensity, until it reaches the top of the sphere, at a very grayed point near the neutral pole. Only one hue would be strong of dark value; the second hue would be of a moderate intensity, but of a lighter value, and the third hue would be lighter still and very close to the neutral pole. Never use these widely-separated colors together in strong and equal intensity, at least in hooked rugs.

Triads do not have the simplicity of a monochromatic harmony, nor the close relationship of an analogous harmony, nor the pleasing contrast of a complementary harmony. It is like bringing three people of widely-different personalities together for an evening. It is only as two are willing to let the third take the lead, that the evening will be successful. Otherwise, if all wish to hold the attention of their hostess, she would indeed be in difficulty.

Personally, I think the triads are best used in geometrics or conventional designs.

LUSEBA

A DOUBLE complementary harmony was chosen for "Luseba" hooked by Louise Hopfman, Teacher, of Lancaster, Mass., Sally Newhall, Teacher. Mrs. Hopfman has carefully identified the colors, and graciously offers them to you. If you have taken the Color Course, you can refer to your color cards. Her outer background is an extremely grayed medium light yellow (Y 6/2). The inner background is like deep Old Ivory over white (Y 7/2).

The circle at the center is outlined with very dark grayed red, such as you might get with extremely strong Taupe dye over white (R 3/1), which is repeated for the underside of each swirling petal, and the center is filled with a mottled shade of extremely grayed darker yellows. The petals of the swirling center are developed in an alternate manner, one changing from dark to medium values (R 3/2, R 3/4 and R 4/4), such as you might get from adding a little Scarlet to Taupe over white for the first, combining Cardinal and Mahogany over tans for the second, and strong Mahogany over white for the third. The next one changes from medium to light values (R 4/4, R 5/4 and R 6/4), repeating (R 4/4) from the first group and combining tints of Cardinal and Gold over white for the second, and Mahogany over white for the third. You will note that the light values are fingered well back from the tips, and run along the overlying curve of each petal.

The scrolly leaves are very dark grayed blue-greens (BG 3/1, BG 4/2, BG 5/1, BG 5/2), Jade over medium dark gray for the first, Green over medium gray for the second, weak Myrtle Green over medium gray for the third, and weak Green over white for the fourth. Mingled with them is a very soft grayed Violet, PB 5/1, such as you might get from weak Navy over medium gray. Notice that the darker values are used in excess of the lighter values. The brighter and lighter values at the extremities are fingered well back into the scroll. The scroll is veined with the varied reds.

The "S" scroll that forms a small and unimportant border is of medium and lighter values of the reds, and they are veined with the varied blue-greens. Their charm lies in their variation, one from another, thus avoiding any set and hard effect.

Although the background and the Mahogany reds are on the warm side, the large area covered by the blue-green scrolly leaves makes a good balance of warm and cool hues.

MECCA

[104]

THE MAIN point to keep in mind in any Oriental is to choose about three colors, but several values of each, and use one hue in greater quantity than the other two. Small amounts of a neighboring hue of one of them may serve as enlivening outlines.

"Mecca," hooked by Mary Benson of Detroit, Michigan, Julia B. McGuire, Teacher, is a split complement of R, B and G. The main hue is a dark, dull American Beauty material, "as is," used in the center background, and in the background of the second and fifth borders. Other reds, in the form of paisley and a small navy and blue plaid served as fillers in small detail of the turtles in the wide border, as outlines of the birds in the first and fourth borders, as small fillers in figures in end panels, and in other small accents.

The blues range from a bright navy, a slightly greenish dark, bright blue and several values of old blue grading up to a very light one. Navy was used for two lines at the edge of the rug and the backgrounds of the third border and two end panels. The light blues were used as fillers for the birds in the first and fourth borders (outlined with American Beauty), and the comb surrounding the turtle in the second border (outlined in Maize). The medium and light blues were also used for a filler of the "S's" in the fifth border (outlined with creamy beige) for varied fillers or outlines in small detail in the two end panels, and for three lines each for the pyramid border.

The greens range from dark to light, the darkest being two black and white small checks and fine plaids, dyed in Bronze Greens, the medium dark being Reseda over gray, and a medium light plain green, "as is." The greens were used for the fillers of the turtles (outlined in light green), the buds in the third border, the Tree of Life and for the lantern at the peak of the pyramid.

The neighboring hue of old gold (brown and white trousers dyed in Old Gold) and maize, "as is," were used for single lines to separate the three different blues of the pyramid border, and for accents and outlines in the small detail. Creamy beige was used for the backgrounds of the first and fourth borders, and around the pyramid.

Thus, one of the hues covers the largest areas or larger details, but all three were used as varied outlines or fillers in detail, thus lending repetition and continuity, and binding them together as a whole.

CHILCOTT LEAVES

ACANTHUS SCROLL

GREEN was to be the dominating color (although the color plan was a triad), in "Chilcott Leaves" hooked by Mrs. Grace Lesser of Springfield, Vt., Teacher. Mrs. Lesser gives credit to Mrs. Harrison G. Otis, Teacher, with whom she had corresponded regarding her color plan. I am always thrilled when one teacher graciously bows to another!

The three hues used were Y (weak Gold, Golden Brown, Mummy Brown, Bronze and Seal Brown to give parchment gold), G (Reseda Green, Aqua Green and Dark Green) and RP (Magenta, Rose and Terra Cotta for a varied soft mauve). Seven values of grays were used for all three hues. Each dye was used separately and also mixed with others to secure a wide variety of shades and tints. Medium and medium dark grays were crowded into the dyepot of the green dyes for a mottled background.

The largest plume-like scrolls were of the greens, very dark at the base and light at the tips. The small end and corner leaves were a soft mauve shade, tipped with delicate gold. The intervening leaves between the two were of the parchment golds, shadowed with Mummy Brown and blended into tints of the dyes of the first group, with some of the mauve fingered in near the veining. The color of one set of leaves or scrolls was carried forward to one of another kind, in subtle shadows or delicate highlights, to give repetition and unity to the color plan as a whole.

VARIOUS checks and plaids were used in certain areas of "Acanthus Scroll" hooked by Mrs. Harold Pederson of Wollaston, Mass., Marjorie S. Thompson, Teacher. They are used as fillers in certain areas of the knobby ends which break away from the main part of the scroll, the latter being in grayed greens and dull greenish-golds. The plaids vary, one being of green, white, orange and brown check, another of red, brown and white check, still another of green, white and brown plaid, each one being carried forward from one detail to another, thus giving continuity to the scroll as a whole. The outer background is navy, and the inner background a light beige. The roses are made from a combination of Cherry, American Beauty and a little Gold dye, which gives them a slightly Terra Cotta tone. All the foliage is of blue-greens.

Variations of Color Harmonies

The wonderful thing about color is that after you understand its law and order, you may combine any colors you wish, *if* you follow certain fundamental principles.

You may combine your harmonies in various ways. For instance, as suggested under Monochromatics, you can swing slightly to one side or the other, picking up a small amount of analogous hues to give the development much more interest, and yet keep the feeling of simplicity to its general plan. You may combine analogous harmonies with a touch of the complementary of one of them, thus bringing a cool or warm balance into your color scheme. Or, in a complementary color harmony, you could pick up a neighbor of one of the complements.

Or you may combine *any* of the hues to suit your fancy, *if* you will remember the circles of intensity. Thus, complementary may be combined with near complement, as in pre-

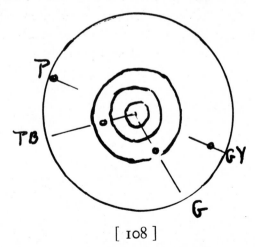

vious sketch, but use the latter (PB and G) in more moderate intensities, as indicated by dots in circle of intensity.

Or an analogous harmony may introduce a little of its three complements, but let them be subtle and of lower intensities. Decide which of the hues is to be most intense and subdue the others, by varied weaker intensities, as in this sketch.

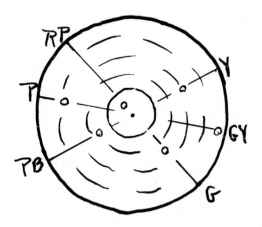

A practical example of this could be a GY scroll with accents of stronger G, and edges of a more subdued Y, with flowers of moderate Y and varied grayer shades of RP, P and PB.

A variation in the application of several values in each of the colors used will give additional interest. Thus, one detail might blend from very dark to medium values, another detail might be predominantly of medium values with very little dark values, while still another might have more light values with very little medium value.

"GEORGE WASHINGTON SCROLL," hooked by Estelle Kemp of Braintree, Mass., Teacher, was created for a pine-paneled living room in which are contrasted the warm hues of reddish-browns and cool blue-greens. The design has a historical interest because the motifs were taken from the wallpaper in George Washington's bedroom at Mt. Vernon. The draperies are in mahogany, dusty rose and dusty pink, with a gold tracery design woven in the cloth in an all-over effect.

Drab tans and dull browns were dyed Mahogany, and mottled with strong Egyptian Red to liven their character for the outer background. The inner background was a light gray, with a mere suggestion of green in it. Weak tints of Jade and Terra Cotta dyes were spooned here and there to produce a delicately mottled effect. Their tints were made apparent in the hooking by making irregular patches of first one and then the other, always surrounding these little islands with the soft gray, "as is," so that the tints melted away into the background.

Tans and beige scraps of varied types of woolens were dyed many values and shades of Egyptian Red, Mummy Brown, Mahogany, Rust and Old Gold for the scroll, which blended from dark, rich Egyptian Red and Mahoganies into lighter Rusts and Golds along the outer edges, where they lie against the dark background. The exaggerated veining of deep aqua was flanked with pale green. Both materials were "as is" fabrics, and were repeated in the penny detail of the scroll.

The harp or lyre was developed in Old Golds, tinged with a bit of Rust, blending into pale Gold highlights at the center, and was edged with the deep Mahogany. The trumpets were formed from the light, rusty shades of the scroll. In the vine, blue-green leaves blended into yellow-green highlights, while yellow-green leaves blended into blue-green highlights. Both were veined with the varied mahoganies. Notice how the directional line of hooking in the body of the scroll makes it roll over. Notice, too, the feathery effect in the way the colors appearing around the veins were fingered into others. The penny detail, with its scintillating stronger intensities of aqua and green, gives a jewel-like effect to this detail.

SEVEN SISTERS

BLYTHE SHOALS

"SEVEN SISTERS," hooked by Doris Reich of Schenectady, N. Y., Alice Dodd, Teacher, was made for a bedroom with a treasured old canopy bed, flounced and ruffled with point d'esprit. The flower colors repeated those from one wall, and the other plain pink walls were enhanced by the rich blackish-purple outer background of this rug (Plum and Cherry, well spotted over pink). It had been dyed unevenly, so there was a variation in its values, and occasionally one gets the glint of a stronger intensity. The inner background had been stripped of its color, and very slightly tinted with a suggestion of Chartreuse, to give an acid yellowish effect. The teacher pays her pupil the compliment of getting the most exotic colors from her dyepot, having vision and imagination to use them in just the right places.

The scroll is large and dominant, and in hooking it she wished to complement the RPs of the floral center. So a variety of YGs (Myrtle Green and Buttercup Yellow over a variety of materials) gave the variations desired. The curved directional line of hooking gives additional contour, following the veining, or swinging out to make the scroll curve and curl. It was veined in a wide variation of Rs (Garnet, Cardinal, Crimson and Cherry), darkest in shadowed areas, with delicate tints in its highlights.

The rose is of varied reds, the tulip of Garnet, Plum and Mulberry over pink. For the pansies and morning glories, the same dyes were used over blue. White in the other two flowers provides contrast, the wild rose blending into Wild Rose shadows, and the lily into Chartreuse, with palest tints of Crimson.

EVEN THE dishes of her dining room, which featured pale pinky mahogany and grays, were used as the color plan of "Blythe Shoals" hooked by Elsie Rathbun, Teacher, of Norwood, R. I., under Dorothy Gailey, Teacher.

Her background was extremely dark, of a very grayed reddish wine (Wine and Maroon over medium tans).

The scroll in lighter values and extremely grayed intensities was developed from varied grays, "as is," in its main body (veined with very dark Taupe) and blended into grayed mahoganies in the side curls, accented with mahogany pink at their tips, reflecting the floral colors within. The iris of mahogany pinks was brighter than the other flowers. A tulip of the grays from the scrolls was pinky mahogany on the inside of the petals. The Canterbury bells shaded from the mahogany pinks into orchids, but the inside of their cups were the grays of the scroll. The foliage varied, some of it blended from yellow-greens into blue-green turnovers, and other leaves were of blue-greens with mingling accents of yellow-greens.

RICHMONT SCROLL

A VARIED color harmony was safely planned in the very grayed colorings in "Richmont Scroll" hooked by Gretchen Barkhuff of Wethersfield, Conn., Teacher. It includes several hues, but they were all muted except the R of the roses.

The outer background is a dark antique green (Dark Green over dark oxford gray), contrasted with a much lighter inner background of grayed BG (a light tint of Myrtle Green), the latter reflecting the Williamsburg green of her wallpaper and woodwork.

The largest outside scrolls are in many values and intensities of BG (Myrtle Green and Turquoise Green over varied greens and grays), and the smaller side scrolls turned to a light grayed green where they tilt toward the center. They are all veined with varied reds (Maroon and Mahogany dyes), which are repeated in varied values in the segmented branch.

The small inner scrolls are grayed green (Reseda), being less striking against the lighter background, but have accents of stronger BGs at their tips, thus relating them to the outer scroll. They are veined with yellow.

The large center rose — the focal point of interest — is of gay Rs (Maroon and Mahogany), echoed in slightly softer intensities in those in the outer area. It is repeated in the veins of its leaves, which are also spot-dyed with R, and used as shadows in the yellow padulas. The fluted flowers are muted Orchid, carried forward to the shadows of the white lilies, in the morning glories and in the center of padulas. The yellow of the padulas forms yellow stamens in the white lilies, and the veins of their leaves. All these colors repeat the small flowers of the wallpaper of the room in which the rug lies. Thus, the center rose is reflected several times, the blue-green complementing it in grayed shades in large areas.

The leaves of the lilies are a bright green (Mint Green and Green); the elongated leaves are Reseda with yellow veins.

All-Color Harmony

It is possible to use *all* the hues in harmony, but it must be done with great care. Therefore, the only safe path from one hue to its opposite is an elliptical path, through the Color Sphere and back again, like the following sketch.

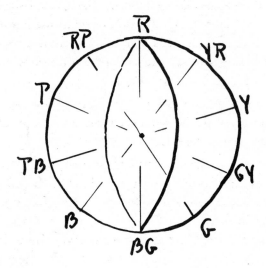

The elliptical path may travel horizontally (all through the same value) from one hue across to its opposite, but as you leave the first to cross the wheel, all the intervening hues begin to hug the neutral pole more closely, the grayest being half way across.

The elliptical path may also travel diagonally from a dark value of bright intensity of one hue, through the intervening hues of gradually lighter values, but gradually duller intensities, to the center, where they are grayest, and thence growing gradually brighter and still lighter to its opposite hue, thence returning through gradually duller intensities and slightly darker values, to the center on the other side of the neutral pole, and then gradually growing brighter and darker to its place of beginning.

Thus, you can plainly visualize that as you leave one hue, R, for instance, in its outer area of intensity, to cross to BG, all the intervening hues on the warm side begin to hug the neutral pole (that is, grow extremely grayed, the grayest being at Y and GY). All the cool hues become extremely grayed, the grayest being at P and PB. From a practical point of view, this means that only your Rs and BGs would be the brightest (and one of these should be brighter than the other). Then all other colors (or as many as you decide to use between these two) must be quite soft and grayed. Of course, the diagonal path, using many values and of varied intensities, would be my choice in creating hooked rugs.

The wide choice of colors you would have under an all-color harmony would be better visualized by a study of the all-color dye wheel, herein.

When you can *harmoniously* bring *all* hues into a design, you have created a most interesting and delightful effect, but it is difficult to do. There are pitfalls to watch for, which apply especially to hooked rugs. For instance, when you combine all hues, without regard to their values and intensities, your rugs could become loud and discordant. The more hues you use, the greater the need for moderation. The larger the area (such as background), the greater the need for weaker intensity. Keep these additional points in mind:

Let but *one* hue dominate all others. It may be in its intensity, applied to certain flowers, or in more moderate intensity, and in larger areas to such details as a scroll. In a geometric, its intensities may be applied to certain smaller detail, or in more moderate intensities to its larger areas, such as background. Let all other hues be in the softer and more grayed shades, so one hue will not vie with another.

Let one value dominate, either in background, scroll or the largest of the main flowers; or in the case of a conventional, geometric or Oriental design, in the larger areas.

Carry the hue of one flower (or detail) over into accents (or detail) of another. The hues of a rose may be used as the shadows of a tulip; the hue of the tulip as accents in a lily, etc. Or in the case of a geometric or Oriental, the hue used as the filler of one small detail may be used as an outline for another. In this way, the repetition of all the hues, even though in small areas or accents, will give rhythm to your color plan and bind all colors together in unity.

In any all-color harmony, you may use *any* range of values in the varied detail of a design. While the all-color dye wheel on page 284, which crosses from an intensity of RP–R to G–BG, shows a range of medium to dark values — the choice of values is your own. The important point is that the intensities be confined to the grayer shades as you swing away from your dominant color through the intervening colors around the wheel. Thus your range of values might include all the lighter values which run right to the top of the pole — or the still darker ones which start at its base — or a combination of any of them, in such skips as please your fancy! These additional values do not necessarily have to be applied too often — but used rather to develop certain detail in accordance with your desires.

Looking again at the dye wheel it will be easy for you to visualize the larger areas of this all-color harmony in the grayer shades of G–BG (the complement of RP–R), the intensity of RP–R in the important flower of a bouquet (if it is not too large), the hues lying nearest to the latter in the less important floral detail, and the hues lying nearest to the G–BG for possible scrolls which usually cover a rather large area.

Thus, once you understand the law and order of all color, you can move about smoothly through the thousands of colors which are available to you, step by step, in any value or intensity of one hue, or step by step into similar values and intensities of neighboring hues, but the steps of intensity from one hue to another are easiest made in those which lie adjacent or close to the neutral pole.

Yet, in cases where emphasis is necessary, especially in certain geometrics or orientals, a dramatic effect may be secured by the use of small amounts of bright intensity of widely-separated colors.

GARDEN'S GIFT

A DELIGHTFUL all-color harmony was developed in "Garden's Gift" hooked by Ethel H. Bruce, Teacher, of Haverhill, Mass., in Sally Newhall's Teachers' Class. It includes a white flower in each row as suggested in the Dye Dabbler covering this design. Its background of dark, dull and slightly khaki-ish green (from Bronze, Old Gold and a bit of Black over taupe material) proved a perfect foil for its lovely coloring.

The vine border is a very subdued greenish parchment color, graying down light bright green by spotting it with weak Strawberry, and also an Olive Green spotted with weak Strawberry, Mummy Brown and Myrtle Green.

Many of the colors in the fifteen different flowers were dyed together to give them an overtone. The tiger lily, carnation and wild rose are the brightest and are of similar coloring, secured from Rose, Strawberry and Burgundy dyes. The rose is a little lighter value and softer intensity, and slides a little into a grayed coral pink.

The rusty-peach hibiscus made from Peach, Apricot and Bronze has a thumb print of dull purplish-blue (Blue over Gray, spotted with Garnet), which is outlined with Maroon, Plum and Bronze Green.

The zinnia and daffodils repeat a peachy coloring but with Old Gold and Bronze added.

One of the ruffled petunias is a soft orchid — the other a purplish-blue — the former being repeated in one of the pansies, and the latter in the morning glories — yet the second pansy also picks up a little of the golds from the zinnia, while the morning glory also has a delicate highlight of a pinkish-white.

The white flowers add an interesting note to the entire development, having varied colored accents. The magnolia has turned petals of soft grayed orchid pinks from the roses; the narcissus has a center cup of gold; the dogwood has a grayed orchid cast in its shadows; the daisies have a bluish-white shadow and the dahlia has pinkish-lavender shadows.

All the foliage has been played down into the background by being developed of extremely subdued shades of green.

Teachers' Annual Exhibit, 1953

"SYLVAN SCROLLS," hooked by Helen Read of Sharon, Mass., Teacher, features an all-color harmony with RP dominating in the background, to bind it to a mulberry-rose broadloom carpet. The background varies from a medium mulberry (two parts Rose and one part Mulberry over light and medium gray), within the outer row of scrolls, to a darker shade outside the scroll (one part Rose to two parts Mulberry over dark gray), with blackish mulberry for the edge. Most of the outer scrolls blend in a vertical path of G, from dark base to light tips, dyed over light blue and light gray materials, obtaining several values. The exception is in the two end scrolls, which shades from a blackish-mulberry, sinking into the background, to a tint at the tips. Some of the inner scrolls blend from G base to extremely grayed shades of dyes from the areas of YG, Y, R and RP. Others turn the other way, from G into dyes from the area of B, PB, P and RP, and all of them are dyed over "oatmeal" material. Some are spotted, too, with dyes of one of the other hues. The tips of many of the scrolls turn to tints of the color next to them. Thus, a mulberry scroll blends into a tint of it, and thence into a very grayed greenish-white, if near a green scroll. Mrs. Read repeats the hues of one scroll as veins in another. When it is necessary to use the complement of the color at the tips, she spots oatmeal materials with tints of both colors to make the transition from one into the other.

"Dowry Needlepoint" (right above), hooked by Gloria Rindge, Ware, Mass., Gladys Skiffington, Teacher, is a varied color harmony, including P, RP, R, YR, Y and GY. The P is strongest and begins to take an inward path around the neutral pole, growing stronger at the extremity of GY. The background is a very dull, dark mahogany red in the outer area, with a light beige background under the medallions. The little borders around the medallions and at the edge of the rug are three lines — gray, gray spot-dyed with flower colors and white spot-dyed with flower colors. White daisies, with gold accents, red-purple tulips, mahogany fantasy flowers and brownish roses are the main flower hues. Yellow-greens and Bronze form the leaf detail.

The "Dowry Needlepoint" (left above), hooked by Mrs. Payson Reed of Whitinsville, Mass., Eleanor Loftus, Teacher, has a blackish-maroon background in the medallions, with a lighter weak maroonish-gray background around the medallions. Much of the floral detail was in the reds and red-purples, but there was at least one, if not two, whitish flowers in each block including the daisies of extremely soft bluish-white, with taupy shadows. The foliage was spot-dyed blue-greens and yellow-greens, in such a manner as to make them sink away into the extremely dark background.

Ceres

THE COLOR scheme in "Ceres," hooked by Mrs. William Connlley Ousler of Marianna, Ark., Mrs. C. Malone Battle, Teacher, was inspired by a beautiful fruit painting by Claude Monet.

The outer background was an extremely low intensity of medium dark Reseda Green dyed over beige, and the inner background a tint of the same dye over white. Against this, the subtle scroll was played down into the background through very dull Bronzy Greens, blending sometimes into Bronze knobs and tips, repeating the Bronze tones from the cornucopia and basket, and other times shading into weak tints of the fruit colors. Where the latter colors were complementary to the scroll, spot-dyed materials of both the greens and reds were used for the area of transition necessary before blending into the colorful edges of the scroll.

The cornucopia and basket were a vertical gradation of dull Old Gold, blending into Bronze shadows.

The fruits were dominantly plum, peach and gold, with an outstanding development of taupy white melon and grapes, both of which had greenish shadows (tints of Reseda and a pinch of Old Gold), with white highlights. The pineapple was blended of dull Rust Brown, with a pinch of Old Gold, and was of very minor importance in color. The apples were varied, some being dark Maroon, some a light, soft YR, highlighted with gold, and others a rather light Bright Green with a pinch of Reseda added. The plums were a soft violet. The peaches were dyed in Crimson, and then dipped in weak Violet, thus being a reflection from the plum, while their blushes were of Violet over pink material. The pears were beautifully shaded in blends of Peach, Golden Brown, Maize and Old Gold. The strawberries (being a small area) took on more intensity in deep Crimson, while an occasional unripe one repeated the white of the grapes. The cherries were Cardinal, with an occasional extra highlight of pinky white.

All the foliage was of varied values and intensities secured from Reseda, Bronze Green and Bronze.

Thus, as you follow these varied hues around your Color Wheel, you will identify this as an all-color harmony, but extremely subtle, because of the low intensity of the greater area of the design.

Now Mrs. Ousler's rug will have a distinct relationship to the lovely Monet painting in her dining room.

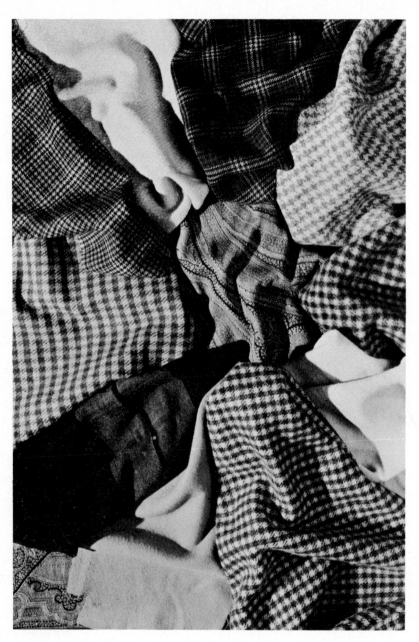

Texture

The mixture of textures, paisley, plaids and checks with plain materials will produce a much more interesting effect, especially in scrolls.

Ten Pertinent Points

Now let's consider some features, each one of which is of great importance in a good hooked rug.

1. MATERIALS AND TEXTURES

Limitation of material should be no deterrent in planning your rugs. Even when you are limited to a lot of one color, you can still secure an unlimited amount of color from it, if you are willing to experiment with taking the color out of it by boiling in sudsy water, or with Color Remover, and dyeing over it. Spot-dyeing over a colored material, for instance over varied blue materials, will give you some delightful scroll colors to work with. Try Burgundy, Magenta, American Beauty and even Apricot, Peach and Coral over the lighter values of blue, and see what delightful effects you can get. Because the basic color is blue, all these can be used together in making a painted scroll. You will discover others yourself!

When imagination is used in the use of your materials "as is," you can secure some delightful effects. It is only as you are willing to play with your materials, hooking them in even to the point of being willing to rip out afterward, that you can secure some most unusual effects.

Personally, I think a scroll of materials "as is," if you have the proper colors, values and intensities, can be as delightful as anything which you may dye. Make a practice of collecting old materials, and I say "old," because they will have become softened by time and cleansing and still have a lot of wear in them to create a delightful scroll. It will take time, but make a practice of storing all your different colors in separate boxes. Save one good-sized piece, and pin those of each color together, grading them according to value or intensity. When you get ready to make a scroll, you will have a wide assortment of materials to work with, without benefit of dye.

One of the loveliest scrolls I have ever seen was made under Mrs. R. G. Stearns, Teacher, of Portland, Maine, from just such a collection of gray materials, combined with tans. One part of the scroll in a "Goddess of Fortuna" was developed in the grays, and the other part in varied tans. The greens of the foliage, repeated in the veining, produced a delightful effect.

A variation in color, value, intensity and *texture* (such as checks, plaids, herringbones and mixtures) is quite important in a geometric design. An accumulation of materials "as is" may be utilized in this way. No matter what the intensity, value or texture, if it falls within a certain hue (dependent upon your color plan) it can be used. Thus, if you have saved all sorts of tans, beiges, warm browns, pinky tans, yellowish-tans, rusts and golden browns, in a wide variety of materials, plain and mixed, they would make a delightful combination with a group of Gs of the same type of mixtured materials. The same would be true of any other near complements, that is, neighbors of any two complements.

2. BACKGROUNDS

The background of a hooked rug is THE MOST IM-PORTANT FEATURE to be determined before you begin to hook. But let's reason it out to see just why.

Webster's International Dictionary gives this definition of background: "That which is back of anything and against which it is viewed." In other words, its main reason for being is to bring out the beauty of the detail which is in the foreground. Now don't LOSE SIGHT OF THAT FACT!

Probably the most common question of a teacher to a pupil is: "What are you planning for your background?" and probably the usual answer is: "I haven't decided yet." Yet this is truly the most important decision to make when you start to hook a rug. Once this is decided, you will know what you are going to play your colors against. It will save you a lot of time in pulling out and correcting colors later, if you will not only make the decision as to your background, but hook a small area of it around your varied details, as you develop them, so you can see exactly how its hue, value and intensity are going to appear against that particular background.

Naturally, in planning your rug, the background should have some connection with the room where it is to be used. If a light rug is desired, choose some light value from the wall, its paper or the background of the drapery. If the rug is to be a dark one, choose some dark, dull shade from some important piece of furniture, or other dominating detail of the room. A tint of a dominating color of a room also makes a good background. That gets you off to the right start, for then the general tone of your background will tie up to your room. Of course, if the rug is going to be before a fireplace, or be the one important rug in the room, and therefore draw considerable attention, the background has a new consideration. For instance, if it lies upon a broadloom carpet, it will have a closer relationship, and sink away into the carpet, somewhat, if the background is of a slightly lighter or slightly darker value, or a slightly brighter or a slightly weaker intensity of the same hue as the carpet, so the two flow together. On the other hand, if it lies upon a polished or waxed floor before a fireplace, and you wish to dramatize it, the background can take on more interest.

Keep the following fundamentals in mind:

The general value of your background affects your detail. Thus, a black background may make light hues of moderate intensity appear weak and whitish because of the *strong contrast* between the *values* of background and detail, which overpower the hue and intensity. You should use more of the middle values of strong intensities to give your color plan strength.

But an off-white or an extremely neutral background

would make the same colors appear much brighter. So, if your intensities are not too strong, the detail would show off better against a light background than an extremely dark one.

Details of dark values will appear darker upon a very light valued background. Thus, a real dark blue flower against a very light grayed background would appear much darker than the same blue flower would against a dark gray background.

When your background and detail are similar in values, the detail is lost against the background. This is so often the case, and usually happens because ruggers will put in their detail first, without any thought of what they are going to use for the background. Then, as an example, if the colors in their floral detail are not too strong and of medium values, and they should happen to choose a medium value background, all the detail is lost against the background because the values are so nearly balanced where they meet. To correct this problem without too much pulling out, darken or lighten the value at the edge of the detail, or strengthen its intensity.

Likewise, details of very light values will appear much lighter when played upon a very dark or black background than when they are used against an extremely light one. Thus, a delicate pink flower appears much more delicate against black than against a light neutral.

If you wish to dramatize light detail, by all means use it against an extremely dark or black background, but use a fairly strong intensity of color, and avoid the pure white flowers, unless they are saved by intermediate values of green foliage.

Backgrounds are more subtle when there is a variance or a slight fluctuation in their tones, such as you secure by spot-dyeing, or when two or more materials of close hues, values and intensities are mottled, for then they will mingle and produce a delightful effect when hooked. Thus, two or more *slightly* different navys, or greens, or browns, or blacks, as the case may be, produce a much more interesting effect than one would, especially if you distribute them evenly, by rotating from one to the other as you hook.

Avoid sharp differences in the shades or intensities of background materials. Never make *definite* designs or details of them. It may be distracting to the eye, especially if their values are very contrasting.

It is often quite necessary to sink your detail, such as a scroll, into your background, if too much attention is not desired. In that case, have very little difference in the value of your background and the value of the body of your scroll, except for what might be necessary at the tips or curling knobs, to save it. Thus, a somewhat neutral gray scroll of very low intensity of color can be played against a slightly darker background of the same neutral or low intensity hue, relying for interest on lighter values in the twirling knobs or the curling tips, in extremely soft shades or tints of a color. This suggestive color at the tips of the scroll, together with colorful veins, will save it from the background. In fact, playing a scroll down against a background of the same general color creates a delightfully subtle effect. Only a little difference in the values or the intensities of the two hues are necessary to save one from the other. For additional interest, where it is necessary to pull it away from a background of the same color, or to give a new note of interest, try developing leafy projections from a scroll with either analogous or complementary hues of weak intensity. A good example of this development may be found in Dye Dabbler #72, treating the scroll of "Memoria."

As a rule, a strong intensity is seldom used as background because it would then have the tendency to make the detail appear secondary. The exception to this rule is where you use the somewhat neutral or extremely low intensities in your details, and rely upon color in your background to give it interest. #563, "Woodland Sprite," was developed in this way in "Dye Dabbler" #62 where an extremely dark and somewhat rich red was used for a background and all the leafy detail

OLLIVIA

THE BACKGROUND in "Ollivia," hooked by Mrs. Alexander Johnston of Worcester, Mass., Teacher, is an extremely dark yellowish-green with slightly mottled effect. It was a worn blanket of faded black and ivory squares, dyed in Olive Green and Dark Green. It was irregularly hooked in a directional line across the rug.

The scroll is played down and is made up of all sorts of browns, from very dark to lighter soft browns and taupe, with very few highlights of a "tanny" taupe. It is veined with paisley.

The important part of the detail is the flowered center, in which Maroon reds have been used for the chrysanthemums, blending into rose and soft pink, with extreme highlights, almost white, at the tips of the petals. Repeating deep brown, from the scroll, in the center of one, and yellowish tones in the other avoided monotony. These browns and yellowish tones were repeated again in the lilies, with lighter values and more yellow in those at the two ends. The tulips are of three colors, each cluster having one of white with gray shadows, one of rose-pink and one of plum, the latter two with white highlights. The plum tulip shades back into a very light, almost white base; the rose-pink tulip is a tint of Maroon and has the darker values on the inside of the petals; the white tulip has a grayed yellow-green center petal. The five-petaled flowers near the center are white with grayed plum shadows, repeated from the tulips. To these she added some turned-over petal accents of soft violet with flecks of pink fingered in to make them look like wild roses. The rosebuds were deep maroon.

All the foliage was of varied greens, but strong enough or light enough so they would not be lost in the green background, and are veined with the varied browns from the scroll. The tulip leaves were quite a contrasting light blue-green, and held their own nicely against the mossy green background.

A high point of interest in this rug is the fact that Mrs. Johnston has successfully superimposed a profusion of green foliage against a green background, losing no definiteness of character.

was worked out in neutral grays or extremely low intensities of color. The one other bright intensity was in the tiny bright blue berries of the woodbine because they covered such a small area.

It is not always easy to see the possibilities of weak colors and neutral materials in the detail of a design. Gene Cheshier of Anchorage, Kentucky, Teacher, was in the middle of her Color Course when she received the Dye Dabbler on "Woodland Sprite," and set about to put the lesson to work. She writes: "I didn't see how they could ever make a very colorful rug. But it's one of the most admired rugs I own. The gentlemen particularly go for that deep, rich red background." It was much admired at our 1952 Exhibit.

But if a background is well covered with details of a design, especially in one like the "Cat's Paw," #207, illustrated herein, stronger color may be used in the background, if it is balanced by larger areas in weak or moderate intensities. Thus, the background of this design might be a rich garnet because so little of the background shows. The paws and striped border, being the greater area, might be of moderate intensities, in the middle to lighter values of the same hues, or of a combination of hues in certain color harmonies.

Incidentally, not too many people realize that this design was copied from an old rug, which is now owned by me. It is said that a Sea Captain originated the pattern, having been inspired by the little whirling patches made by the wind upon the sea. The old rug has a background of lovely rich red, such as strong Strawberry dye. The little irregular marks between the paws are like Khaki Drab. The paws vary, some having outer edges of very bright navy, with inner lines of lighter values of it, and centers of tawny tans, such as you might get from Ecru dye. Other paws have centers of lighter values of Strawberry at the center, while still others include Bronze. The bright navy blue forms the first line in the border, and then each line of hooking in the border is a different value or intensity of the various shades used in the center, which gives

[134]

it a rather "thready" effect. It is really very lovely! Perfect with Early American antiques!

In my copy of the design, I have given a little more irregularity to the contour of each paw. Today it is being developed in a wide variation of colors, some of them having an Oriental effect. It is popular because it is available in three sizes, and also in a stair runner.

In order to avoid the misfortune of running short of background material in a floral and scroll design, it is advisable to keep away from the detail and inner part of the scroll when hooking. If you have to improvise with a material that is not exactly the same shade (especially if it is slightly darker), the darker value can be used, to be fingered into it, and act as a shadow between scroll and center background, and the same is true underneath the floral bouquet.

Remember again your afterimage on backgrounds. If your background is a neutral or nearly neutral, bright colors may throw a complementary cast over the general tone of it. When the neutral background is about the same value as a bright hue near by, the afterimage is even stronger. Of course, if your background is off-white or very light, the afterimage will be quite like the complementary of a bright color used near by. But if the background is a definite color, the hue itself is changed somewhat by the effect of the afterimage, from bright details near by. Thus, a strong GY in detail may throw a purplish cast upon a grayish-blue background.

3. AREAS

The larger areas of a hooked rug design may be the scroll, the floral detail or the background; or, in the case of a geometric or Oriental pattern, they may be in the various units of the design, as well as the background.

The proportion in which you use each color in these various parts or units, and their repetition in the detail of the design, is another very important factor in your color plans.

The theory is that *equality* of proportion, in fact, equality

Woodland Sprite (a pair)

OATMEAL material was tinted with Taupe for the all-over background of the "Woodland Sprite" hooked by Mrs. James M. Robbins of Maplewood, N. J., Mrs. Harry R. McClain, Teacher.

The woodbine leaves were the dominating color, a lovely blue-green (Green dye), veined with Mahogany, its berries of complementary gay Garnet. The oak leaves were the second important hue of Mahogany and Mummy Brown, with acorns of Rust and Dark Brown caps. The hazelnut leaves were a quiet Olive Green with nuts of the Mahogany and Olive Green. In all the leaves, checks were used in dyeing for shadows. Notice the element of surprise in the little white nuts or berries with pale Mahogany tips.

"WOODLAND SPRITE" was hooked by Mrs. Florence Baer of Springfield, Mass., Mrs. Arline Robbins, Teacher.

There were red and yellow accents of color in the hall, in which this rug was used on a dark brown painted floor. The plan was to use warm hues, but to play them against a grayed plum outer background, with brighter shades of it in some of the detail, and a bit of blue to add a cool note to the scheme.

The outer background of very grayed plum was secured by dyeing brown material in Plum dye (1 package of dye to ½ pound of material). The inner background was a yellow material in a weak bath of Bronze dye, which made the two backgrounds complementary, thereby making it necessary to keep the two subtle.

Much of the material in the detail was plaids and mixtures. The oak leaves were made from these, with Violet where it was necessary to lift the detail from the background. The woodbine leaves were made from spot-dyed materials (using Turkey Red, Salmon and Coral), as well as plaids, put through a bath of Terra Cotta. The other leaves were of varied shades, using Bronze, Bronze Green, Olive Green, Reseda Green, Old Gold and Gold dyes. The hazelnuts were white, as well as the little elongated nuts, shadowed with tints from the other colors. The berries were secured from Blue dye.

The corner leaves, you will note, were developed in the manner suggested in Dye Dabbler #60, shading from dark values along one side of the vein to a light edge, and from light values along the other side of the vein to a dark edge.

in all other phases of your color plan, between warm and cool hues, between light and dark values, between strong and weak intensities, is tiresome, and does not tend toward an artistic effect.

As a rule, intense colors, especially of extremely warm hues, should be limited in their areas, while dull hues may be used more generously. Yet there will be exceptions even to this rule, depending on where you are to use the rug. Oftentimes a very gay and rather bright rug appearing in an Exhibit will make one wonder why anyone would use such gay colors in a rug. The answer is often a dark corner, or a cold room which needs this gaiety of color. Therefore, a rug is never at its best, except in the spot for which it was made.

A color plan should always include an area of neutrals or nearly neutrals, that is, very grayed shades of one of your important hues for the eye to rest upon.

Watch out, too, that you do not use light neutral values in too large an area, lest they may exhaust the eye, just as too many low values, unrelieved by strong color or highlights, may depress you.

4. CONTRAST OF VALUES

Generally speaking, most good color plans will have four outstanding values:

> a light value,
> a low value and
> two intermediate values.

Perhaps you have never analyzed a hooked rug design to determine what its areas are. This may take a little practice. Study the design and try to estimate which are the three or four largest areas, the background, the scroll or certain other details in the pattern. As you visualize these areas in light, medium or dark *values*, the development of the rug begins to take place.

Another way to help you visualize what is going to happen when you apply three or four different values to the largest areas of your design is to rough out a small sketch and shade it in with your pencil in these four different values. For instance, suppose you decide upon studying a pattern in which:

> the inner background is the greatest area,
> the scroll is the next largest,
> the floral detail is the third and
> the outer background is the least.

Now, if the inner background seems to you to be almost half of the area of the design, you could rule that off as one in this sketch:

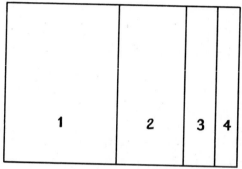

the scroll being the next largest, as two; the floral detail as three; and the outer background as four. Now begin to think of the values you would use in the general development of this design if you applied your darkest values to that outer background which is the smallest area, shading that area in heavily with your pencil, and so on, in the other areas, with gradually lighter shading, so the largest inner area would be the lightest (unshaded). When you get through,

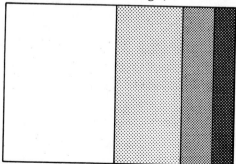

this little shaded sketch will immediately tell you that the greater part of your rug is going to be light or medium light; a small part is going to be medium dark; and a very small part the darkest. Your rug begins to come to life! For one of the first questions to be decided is the general *effect* you wish to secure. Is it to be a light, medium or dark rug? Shading these little rough sketches, after estimating its areas, will help determine this fact.

Now, let us reverse the case, and estimate that a design is made up with:

the darkest value in the larger area
(the entire background),
the lightest value in floral detail and
the intermediate values in the scroll.
The shading of your diagram tells this story.

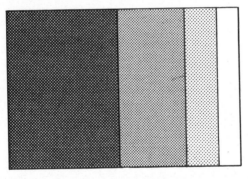

When I say that the intermediate values would be in the scroll, I do not mean that you would be confined to the 4th, 5th and 6th values in the development of the scroll. As a matter of fact, you might have shadows as dark as two or three, and highlights as light as seven or eight, but both these extremes might be applied in small accents, the greater area being in the intermediate values. Thus you can use dark values for accent and light values for highlights and still keep the general development of the scroll as a whole in what one would describe as intermediate values.

Now remember that your lightest value in any color plan

doesn't necessarily have to be the *extremity* of the ninth value (white), nor does the lowest need to be black. Your lightest value can be anywhere between seven and nine, and your lowest value can be as high as three, which would be a medium dark. You will still have the three intermediates of four, five and six for your other two largest proportions. Of course, the closer your values are in the development of your rug as a whole, the more subtle it is. That is, a rug of a medium dark to medium light is quieter, and sometimes more subtle than a rug with an extremely dark outer background and an extremely light inner background, especially if it has a lot of very light and very dark flowers.

Deciding upon the value of the three or four largest areas of your design does not prevent you from using all the values in whatever proportion you desire for the varied detail in the rest of the pattern.

5. BALANCE

The eye is quickly disturbed by lack of balance. It is quite natural for you to go to the window to straighten a curtain or move an object, or turn a chair, or in other ways adjust balance in everything you see.

When I was a little girl, we had a very large and strong "teeter-board," which drew the neighbors' children. My first recollection of balance was that I had to have someone of my weight on the other end if we were to get an even balance. If only smaller tots were playing, it would take two to balance me, and even then one might have to move a little nearer the center to get a good balance.

In developing the details of a hooked rug, color usually flows from the center, which is the natural balancing point. It should receive the strongest color treatment, throwing accent of interest on its dominant detail, unless for some reason the color plan is intended to throw the emphasis to the scroll, and play down the floral detail. Colors equally removed from the center point should balance each other, but the balance may

VERY LITTLE contrast between the general values of scroll detail and background create a subtle effect in this "Memoria" hooked by Mrs. Kenneth Knowles of Oyster Bay, N. Y., Eleanor Loftus, Teacher. The scrolls of neutral grays to white are veined with dull gold, and are played against a grayed old blue background (Copenhagen Blue and Black over a warm gray).

The roses are blended from Maroon dyes; the tulips turn from purples into golds and lilies from taupes to grayed blue throats; violets of deep purples, white dogwood and pussy willows. The colors repeated those in Mrs. Knowles' room, and she says: "They tie the rug to the room in an amazing fashion."

"Young Man's Fancy" (left), hooked by Mary Coggswell of East Weymouth, Mass., Leona Lincoln, Teacher, is made in the color scheme of the Dye Dabbler covering this pattern, which has a blackish-plum background, with pansies of purple, yellow and blue, each having something of the other in it; daffodils of soft yellow with greenish-gold accents; white narcissus and pussy willows, with rope of yellow-green, repeating the foliage hues.

"Young Man's Fancy" (right), hooked by Mrs. Edward E. Shorkey of Palmer, Mass., Aurora Johnson, Teacher, has a teal background, secured from dark gray material that had a yellowish-green fleck, dyed in Green. The pansies were combinations of purple and yellow and yellow and blue, with soft yellow daffodils (Aqualon Yellow, Yellow and Buttercup Yellow over creamy white); narcissus and pussy willows in grays and whites.

The "Frost Oriental" (to the right), hooked by Mrs. Helen C. Ebell of Brookline, Mass., Mrs. Mildred J. Davis, Teacher, utilized a gray coat and one of bright red, with some odds and ends. The gray was dyed both in a series of Maroons and Delft Blues, and the red one was dulled with Terra Cotta and Rust. The varied blues form the greater area of background in the center, and the Rust and soft Golds over the grays were used for the varied detail.

The "Frost Oriental" (to the left) was hooked by Myra Perry of Willimantic, Conn., Teacher. Its main colors are three shades each of very dark, rich reds; light and medium blues (Sky Blue grayed); Old Gold and soft yellow-green, plus Navy, oyster white and some paisley and multicolor plaids. Navy forms the first and third borders and the background of the panel ends. The light and medium blues form the largest areas. The reds, paisley and multicolor plaids are used as fillers and outlines of the smaller detail.

be made like the teeter-board, with one large rose to the right or left of center, balanced by two smaller ones of the same value and general intensity in the opposite direction, or a flower at the upper left may balance another at the lower right.

Equal balances of hues, values and intensities satisfy the eye but are inclined to be uninteresting because the balance is so obvious. In fact, they can sometimes become monotonous.

Uneven balances are more interesting. A small amount of dark color will balance a much larger amount of a light one; a small amount of brilliance will balance a larger amount of weaker or grayed shades, just as it takes a pile of feathers to balance a small piece of lead. Thus, a deep, rich rosebud might balance two large full-blown lighter roses. You may balance any flower of extremely light value by one about one fourth its size in low (dark) value, or any flower in strong intensity will balance several others of much weaker intensity.

Where the design will not adapt itself to this method, the color may be used as exaggerated centers of a flower to bring unity to the color plan. A good example of this will be found in #498, "Persian Ribbon," herein, in which the blue bells which appear at only one end of the floral center are balanced by repeating the blues as the center of the yellowish daisies at the other end. To maintain balance, sometimes only parts of a flower need to repeat a necessary color. Thus blue of a Canterbury bell may be repeated only in the upper petals of a purple pansy or the whites of a wild rose may form the upper petals of a blue iris.

You can obtain balance in your floral corners by balancing them diagonally, if you wish to develop them differently.

An even more interesting balance is the triangular, and in my own original designs, I try to carry out this triangular balance as much as possible, to make it easier for you to maintain a good balance of colors. One rose to the left of center may be balanced by two that are not exactly opposite, but rather in a position to form a triangle, like this.

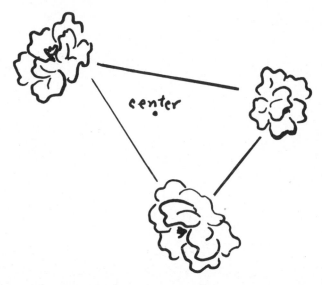

The center of "First and Second Fiddle," #484P, has several triangular balances, as indicated in this sketch.

Notice there are four different triangular balances to satisfy the eye.

When the hues are of unequal intensity, the need for balance is more marked. The *strongest* color becomes *stronger,* the weaker one appears *weaker.*

Here are some other facts to keep in mind in balancing your floral detail:

PERSIAN RIBBON

ROCKLAND SCROLL

ONE OF the best examples of balance is shown in the old-fashioned "Persian Ribbon," hooked by Mrs. Irving Small of Shrewsbury, Mass., Erline Stearns, Teacher. There is but one spray of blue bells appearing on one side in this old-fashioned design. Mrs. Small has made them Aqualon Blue — and to maintain a good balance — repeats this hue as the large centers of the golden yellow daisies which merge into a Terra Cotta base, thus forming a triangular balance. These colors and those in the rest of the floral detail are keyed around the paisley used as a filler for the ribbon in the border which is outlined with the Aqualon Blue.

The roses pick up the general tone of the paisley, being of Egyptian Red shading into Terra Cottas, and thence into many highlights of its tints in some of the petals. Their leaves are all a very dark and somewhat grayed yellow-green, with quite splotchy shadows at their bases, and very exaggerated highlights at their tips. They are veined with the paisley.

The inside background is a light beige, and the border under the paisley ribbon is dark brown.

IN THIS "Rockland Scroll," hooked by Blanche Lewis of Wollaston, Mass., Teacher, the background is a very dark Navy Blue. Its scrolls are RP, of mixtures that give them a little salt and pepper effect when hooked. The general body of the scroll is in the grayer and duller shades, blending out to much lighter soft orchid-pink tints where they meet the background. The accentuated veining is of a rather rich Peacock of dark values where the scroll begins, and lighter values where the scroll lightens.

The center roses repeat the same general hues of the RPs, although one turns slightly more toward rose and the buds are a soft pink. The little flowers around them are white, with extremely soft yellows for accents at the base of the petals, and little lines of Peacock around the centers, with an occasional broken line of color at their edges, where they appear against the dark background.

The rose leaves, like the veining of the scroll, are somewhat glamorized in blue-greens, while the smaller leaves are in even brighter intensities.

[147]

Remember how important it is to have the *contrast of values* in your floral detail. This contrast of values may often appear in small highlights or dark shadows. It is the occasional splashy highlight on a bulging petal that livens up a rose and gives the floral centers life, and the unusual depth in the shadows of the tulip satisfies the eye as to balance.

In small flowers you can secure an interesting, unequal balance of values by developing one or two of a small five-petaled flower in the light values (usually the overlying ones), the other three or four in darker values. This will also help separate one petal from another in these smaller flowers and maintains the individuality of each petal. Three different values at wide intervals, like a very dark value, a medium and a very light value in such a small flower, will often give balance and interest to its development.

Try to keep in mind the common relationship of hues when combining them, especially where you wish to use a light value in one flower and a dark, rich value in another for balance. In a class I noticed a bright R–YR poppy in a rug, and near by it a fuchsia of bright rose pink (RP) sepals, which clashed. I laid a coral pink over the sepals of the fuchsia, and immediately the common relationship of yellow, which was in both the poppy and the coral pink of the fuchsia, brought them into harmony.

If the floral bouquet is large in area, you can use more brilliance in your hues than you can in those of smaller groupings.

Keep also in mind the balance of warm with cool hues in your flowered center. Thus, if you had small flowers like forget-me-nots at each end of a floral bouquet, and the group as a whole was cool, make the forget-me-nots of coral pink instead of blue, or any other warm hue to warm it up. Oftentimes the small groups of small petaled flowers at each extremity of a floral bouquet are different. Balance these by using the same values of possibly two different hues. Thus, a light coral pink in one cluster would balance the same values and intensities with a light turquoise blue at the other extremity.

When using complementaries in small clusters of flowers at the extremities of a floral center, remember that each intensifies the other. Therefore, they should be of about the same value and not too dark a value, and of a moderate intensity. Otherwise they will catch the eye because of their contrast. Flowers of complementary colors may be balanced, too, by using a lighter value of the advancing color to a much larger quantity of the receding color.

Never use a color in one place only, so it appears spotty in the rug. Repeat it in some of the detail and as often as possible.

You can maintain a color balance by using a little imagination in the colors of your leaves, thus repeating some flower hue in an extremely grayed shade may help maintain balance. Of course, in all leaf detail there should be a wide variance in values, in order to give them shadow and highlight.

In scrolls we usually start with the rich, deep or dark shades to flank the veins to give weight to the scroll as a whole, shading into more moderate intensities and values in the intermediate areas, and then into lighter edges. An exception would be where you threw an exaggerated highlight on one side of the scroll near the central vein, shading to a darker edge. After you have worked out the scroll in one corner, your balance is automatically maintained by making the other three the same.

In a repeat pattern of two motifs, strengthen one block more than the other, to get away from equally measured balance.

When balance is lacking, the mind begins to search for what is wrong, for even if you cannot analyze it, you can *feel* it.

6. REPETITION

Repetition is one of the most important words in our

Old Colonial

THE REPETITION of an important color may be applied to both background and detail, as in "Old Colonial" hooked by Phyllis H. Larsen of Washington, D. C., Teacher. The outer background was a mottling of several slightly different teal blues, "as is." The inner background was of lighter value — a similar blue plaid material, over which delicate Ocean Green was spot-dyed, bringing it into closer relationship with the outer area and providing the desired monotone effect.

The large outer scrolls repeated the grayed yellow-greens of the walls of the room, through Turquoise and Chartreuse spot-dyed over sand colored material. The spotty mixture of the inner background provided shadow areas in these scrolls. A delicate Chartreuse outlined the edges and knobs of the scroll. The same colors were used to develop the outer half of the chubby inner scrolls, veining them with Old Rose, while the inner half was blended in light, soft Old Rose, with veins of blue-green. The outer side of the small chain of overlapping leaves was created from the same plaid as the inner background, while the inner side was of a navy from which the color was removed, which left it a grayed blue, similar to the outer background. This gently broke the transition from dark to light background.

You will notice that each cluster of flowers interrupting the outer scrolls is different, and in order to keep continuity, the same general hues are used over and over again. For instance, while all the roses are of Old Rose dye, blending into Mahogany shadows and pinky-yellow edges, some are darker and duller than others. The pansies had Mahogany ears and whiskers with pale pink faces. The white that appears so many times in the flowers, in the outer part of the design, has been repeated in the chrysanthemums in the center (with yellow-green shadows). The morning glories of white have blue-green shadows. The zinnias and smaller flowers were in corny golds and pinkish whites, as were the small flowers in the inner chain, contrasted with leaves of Ocean Green and Turquoise with gold veins. At least one of the flowers in each corner is of creamy white.

All the foliage was developed from combinations of yellow-greens (Chartreuse dye over grays and tans), and blue-greens (Turquoise Green over grays and tans), and was played down more or less in the background.

hooked rug craft! It is only as you repeat colors over and over again, in varied detail, that you give interest and unity to your color plan as a whole. These repetitions do not necessarily cover large areas. Even a line or two, buried among other colors, will satisfy the eye without one really being conscious of them. Thus, if a flowered center had five or six different flowers in the bouquet, try to repeat the color of one flower in some way in another. For instance, a dark, rich red rose might have purple shadows and accents, picked up from the purple shades of a tulip. Tints of the red rose might be used for a wild rose, with shadows of lighter tints of the purple tulip. Tints of the pink wild rose, and also some of the lighter values from the rose, might be used for the raggedy edges of a white carnation. The white of the carnation might be repeated in the highlights of a very grayed lily, with a greenish throat, the latter being a reflection from the foliage greens.

In a pattern like #534, "Sea Grapes," herein, repetition is given through using the same values and intensities in the flat treatment of the grapes as has been used in the shading of the leaf. The veining of the leaf has been carried forward into the heavy stems which separate the units and those of the grapes.

An intermingling of foliage greens will give all leaves more interest. Thus, in a leaf that is definitely BG, shadows of a YG might reflect YG leaves near by. Or vice versa, some of the deep BGs might be brought over into the dark YG shadows. Or, in other leaves, a BG leaf may shade up into a YG tip.

In a geometric, conventional or Oriental design, especially when it is made up of a series of motifs, the main thing to keep in mind is that there must be enough repetition of color to bind all the various units together. Therefore, although each unit should have its own individual distinction, enough of the colors must be carried forward to the other motifs to pull them together into a harmonious whole.

[152]

This is best exemplified by my description of #567, "Filigree," herein, where only two complementary hues are used, but in many values and intensities, combining both hues in each motif, but with a larger proportion of one in the hexagon, and a smaller proportion of it in the intervening motif.

A dominant value may be used over and over again in other details, and the dominant hue in its intensity may be repeated in many small areas; or in its weaker intensity, in the larger areas. All other hues should be repeated several times, or at least as often as possible in the detail of a design, so the eye will carry forward from one detail to another, even though the repetition may be in extremely small areas or minute details.

The color decided upon for a scroll should always have a close relationship to the floral or other colors of the rug. A green scroll, for instance, should repeat the foliage greens from the floral bouquet within. Its veins, knobs and the extremities of its detail offer chances to repeat flower or leaf colors, and thus bind them the more closely together.

7. CONTINUITY

Certain borders call for a feeling of continuity. It is important to carry your general color scheme continuously in a simple and complete manner, in order to give this feeling of continuity. #492, "The Perfume Box," or #538, "Criss Cross," are good examples of this type of border. In the former, two of the bands of one color form three crossing diamonds within an outer border, and then continue on to form the outer border of three crossing diamonds within a second color. It is advisable to use monochromatic or analogous color harmonies in a border of this type, in order to have the two fuse as one. Thus, two different values of one color, or two neighboring colors, for instance, BG in one, with YG in another, would give a feeling of oneness and continuity.

In a repeat border in a pattern like #533, "The Straw-

Teachers' Annual Exhibit, 1950

[154]

CONTINUITY is given to the "Farnsworth Scroll" (lower rug), hooked by Lillian Knight and Ruth Jones of the Hookrafter's Guild, under my supervision, by blending blue-greens into their neighbor yellow-greens, in the scrolls which lie against an antique black background. The corner scrolls are yellow-green, blending into a blue-green section, and thence back to lighter yellow-greens. The inside background is a yellowish cream, darkened slightly under the floral center. All the yellow-greens and blue-greens of the scroll are repeated in the small, unimportant foliage in the center.

The flower tones are mostly in Burgundy and Mulberry shades, but a few have a slightly goldish tone with blue centers, while others pick up a very grayed purplish-blue with mulberry centers. An occasional white flower appears with greenish shadow accents. All the roses and flowers in the two end sprays are quite grayed and medium dark. Thus, the scroll is the important part of this design. The flower colors are repeated in the little segments of the scroll in the corner — darkest in those at the end, and gradually lighter near the tip of the scroll.

Again, by using neighboring hues, continuity is given to "Romantique" (upper left) hooked by Mrs. William Maconachie of Cleveland Heights, Ohio, Eva C. Hruby, Teacher. The underside of the scroll is blended with blue-green tweeds from Reseda dye, and the upperside blends from a dark base of the leaf foliage greens to light tips, veined with rose and plum taken from the floral detail. It lies against an outer background of Plum dye over blue and white checks, and an inner background of light gray tweeds. The roses are from Rose, Garnet and Plum dyes over light gray and white; the tulips and fox-gloves from Rose and Orchid dyes, with Plum shadows, while the chrysanthemums are Gold over light gray and white, with Bronze shadows. The rose leaves are Reseda Green over light gray. The tulip and foxglove leaves are a little greener as some of the material is dyed over a blue-green tweed. All the flower shades have been carried into the leaves for veins. This is a first rug.

Three plaid skirts of varied blues and rose shades form the scroll in the "Duke of Marlborough" (upper right) hooked by Mrs. Frederic E. Charrier of East Hartford, Conn., Mary MacKay, Teacher. They are played against an all-over light gray background. The roses are pale pink, the tulips Maroon and Plum, the chrysanthemums Plum over pink, the cosmos of Maroon and the delphinium of Plum; all of the flowers being "dip-dyed" for gradation.

berry Patch," a slight variation can be given in one frame, from that of another, by a change of values or intensities, or a change of two close neighboring hues, but not to the point of making them spotty, nor interrupting the all-over effect that this design should have.

An unimportant border that serves as a division between flowers, like that in #575, "Garden's Gift," should be played down more or less into the background. While a change in values may give a little additional interest, and help separate one leaf from the other, its development as a whole should be simple, so it will form an all-over effect.

When a scroll is interrupted by certain details, like baskets and cornucopias of fruit, as in #566, "Ceres," carry forward the colors of your scroll into some detail of the cornucopia or the basket, using neighboring hues, which will flow so there will be no sharp jumps. Thus, a YG scroll might turn to knobby ends of soft grayed golds carried forward from the cornucopia or basket.

Continuity can be given by repetition of color, from one detail into another. I've suggested this in many instances through the Dye Dabbler to show you how to bind your separate details together by these little repetitions or flashes of color. It may be maintained, too, through similar VALUES of two hues. You can bind them together best by using neighboring hues.

When a border is made up of several different units and conventional floral details, such as the one in "Amish," maintain continuity by pulling them together through repetition of color and *gradual* changes in values.

When sectional scrolls form a border, as in "Gainsborough" or "Entice," pull them together by using similar hues, values and intensities at their extremities.

In a border like "Bridal Ring," use slightly different values of one hue in the interlocked rings, or if two hues are desired, use neighboring hues.

In a fanciful leafy border, like that in "Dowry Needlepoint," use neighboring hues and close values to keep color flowing. Avoid sharp changes in either color, values or intensities.

In a design like "Rustic Charm," the scrolly leaves appearing between the medallions and along the border serve to pull the various units together. Slight changes in the tips may be permissible for a little interest, but a repetition of colors in each motif to give a *general* feeling of oneness will increase the feeling of continuity.

Watch out for scrolls which crop out from a leaf or flower. Develop them of a hue which "grows away" from the detail gradually (of neighboring or similar hues). There is a feeling of continuity in the transition of neighboring colors.

Be careful in using strong hues in one flower and weak ones in another next to it, because of the contrast, the strong hue becomes stronger and the weak one weaker, thus interrupting continuity.

8. IMAGINATION

Probably there is no part of a hooked rug in which imagination is so important as in scrolls. The "painting" of a scroll is much easier when both colors and varied materials mingle in the dyepot to take on a common relationship, or change gradually in values.

Imagination in floral detail is precious! It is not so much the color you use, as how you use it. It may often be dramatic; it can also be subtle. It is often achieved by the "offshades" which you would not consider realistic, but which create an artistic effect.

Here are seven ways of treating flowers imaginatively, often applied to the queer "padula-like" blossoms that you have difficulty in naming. They are:

1. Blending two colors, so the petals of a flower change from one hue to accents or edges of another hue, like a blue pansy with a reddish-purple edge.

[157]

MOONEY PANSY

ELF'S DELIGHT

IMAGINATION has been truly used in developing "Mooney Pansy" hooked by Mrs. Priscilla Martin of Medford, Mass., Mrs. Ralph C. Wiggins, Teacher. It has a very light background of Silver Gray and a light tint of Wood Rose dyed over white, which gives it a pinkish-gray effect. The outside background is slightly darker. The largest pansy in one corner is of Rust, with lower petals of Rust and Mummy Brown. The second pansy is of equal parts of Rust and Mahogany, and twice as much of Strawberry, with shadow accents in the lower petals of deep Maroon. In the third pansy, the lower petals are extremely deep Mulberry dyed over a black and white check. The opposite diagonal corners are the same. In the two remaining corners the largest pansy is of Rust, Mahogany and Strawberry, and the other two are the same as in the first two corners. In the largest pansies in the center the Mulberries are used, with one of each of the other two combinations. Tints of the Mahogany were carried into the lilies-of-the-valley, and weak Copenhagen Blue grayed with Silver Gray is used for the daisies, with centers of Yellow and Mummy Brown. The foliage is of Olive Green and Bright Green with Rust veins.

"Elf's Delight," an imaginative design in itself, was hooked by Eileen Briggs of Bennington, Vt., Teacher, and was chosen because of her childhood memories of fairies, pixies and May-Day magic. The key to the light mellowed background is Old Ivory over oyster white, spotted with an extremely weak solution of Mint Green to give it an "off-shade." The "star" in her floral center is the jack-in-the-pulpit, which starts with a garnet bathrobe. She discovered it bled in hot water, so she saved some of Jack's "blood" and a little of it went into all other flowers. For other shades in her Jack, she dyed Maroon in several values over various textures. Some of them also went into the pitcher plant. Lighter values of the pitcher plant were carried forward into the ladies' slippers and the wild rose. The color was removed from some pink materials and they were then dyed in a weak solution of Jack's "blood" for the very delicate mallow. The lilies were of Peach, Salmon and Yellow dyes. A textured material was used for the goldenrod (Yellow over gray, and Yellow with Gold over gray). Varied blue materials were injected with Jack's "blood" for the fringed gentian. Violet and Blue over medium blue were used for the purple asters, with tints of Lavender for their highlights, and tints of Lavender and Violet were combined for blue flag and blue bells.

There are twenty-one shades of green in the foliage and ferny border, secured mostly from Dark Green, Reseda, Olive Green, Bronze and combinations of Aqualon Blue, Old Gold, Yellow and Mint Green. Many of them were spotted with the colors from the flowers and with Jack's "blood."

2. Fanciful or off-colors which are difficult to name, like the brownish red-purples of scrub oaks in the Fall.

3. Shading a color from dark to light, with irregular frilly accents of white, like several loops of white interrupting the pale pink ruffled edges of a red petunia.

4. Using green for tints and shadows in white flowers.

5. Dramatizing a flower by strong contrasts of values, like the gay, bright edges of a purplish-blue tulip, which quickly blends down to an almost white base.

6. Using any two contrasting colors with a third intervening one formed by a "marriage" of the two, to bind them together. For instance, blending from a reddish base to a light-blue edge by introducing the intervening hue of purple between the two; or from a bluish base to a delicate yellow edge, introducing a grayed green between the two.

7. Using white for one half a petal on a flower, with grayed hues of a color in the other half.

Imagination instead of reality is used in developing a conventional design of flowers or leaves. A leaf no longer has to shade from a dark base to a light tip, or from a dark center to a light edge. Now the utilization of textures or off-colors used for a filler in this type of leaf, relying upon a contrasting color or value for the edge of the leaf for interest, gives it an Oriental effect. The same would be true of the conventionalized flowers, for here you can play one color against another, without regard to reality. Again the treatment is often flat, relying upon an outlined edge of a contrasting color for interest.

Strive for imaginative blends of color in developing conventionalized detail. This reminds me of a rug which I saw in a Teachers' Exhibit where such a design of leaves was developed in just one flat value of green, yet I knew the teacher was artistic. Later I met the woman who made the rug. She explained to me that her teacher had first developed the leaves in lovely shades from bronze greens into coppers and golds, but that when she took it home and showed it to her husband, he said: "Whoever heard of a leaf in those colors? Leaves are green, just green," and he made her take them out and change them. How difficult it must be to live with one having so little imagination! Even if hooking realistically, use your colors imaginatively.

The important thing is that you are making a rug to tie up to the colors in a room. If you have chosen a leafy design because you enjoy it, or because it is important in that room, and green is not the important color in your room, don't hesitate to use other hues, but in pleasing intensities to carry out the color scheme of your room.

9. EXAGGERATION

Exaggeration is sometimes necessary to give more character to your color plan. It may be in the dominant detail, like a scroll, or in small detail, like flowers and foliage, depending upon the all-over effect you desire.

Exaggerating shadows and highlights in flowers will give a third dimension, as in this tulip, where the extremely dark

rear petals are contrasted with the much lighter petals in the foreground, thus giving you the feeling that there is a space of several inches between the two.

Exaggeration in shadows will aid in giving a well-rounded throaty effect in lilies; or in foxgloves as in this sketch, where the turned back fore petal throws a shadow on the rear of the throat, thus creating a feeling of space.

Likewise, the curled back fore petal also throws shadow on the upper part, also creating the effect that it stands away from it. The same dramatic contrast between darkest values in the shadows and highlights, as applied to small buds, will make you feel you can tuck your finger right into the throat. The edge of the upper part and even the lower rear part of the blossom may have to be a darker value or a little stronger intensity before blending into lighter values to save it from disappearing into the background.

Exaggeration in the directional lines of hooking will give

additional contour to petals, as in those of this rose, where both shadows and intermediate shades swing with each curving line of the petal, blended into lighter values that give the sheen of highlighted bulges.

You can give additional rhythm to the development of a scroll by emphasis of certain lines, with your heavier and darker values. Thus a scroll like #522A, "Pride," might be developed by emphasizing one side of the vein with extremely dark values such as you might get from Bronze Green dye, shading into dark Khaki Drab, thence into light Bronze at the edges of the scroll, swinging your lines of hooking in the directional manner indicated on sketch on page 166. On the other side of the vein, start with a lighter value, which you might get from Ecru, and shade into lighter values of Khaki Drab, and thence into darker values of Bronze, and out to the narrow edge of darker Bronze Green. Naturally, the color development of a scroll like this should always tie in with the foliage colors in the center, and the veining should repeat some of the

GIFFORD AUBUSSON

EXAGGERATION of highlight and shadow give contour to the scrolls of "Gifford Aubusson" hooked by Mrs. Arthur Gress of Edgarton, Wisc., Sarah Leslie, Teacher. The brown of the walnut furniture in the bedroom where this rug lies is the dominating hue in this rug, with Bronze Green and Reseda playing a secondary part. Life and interest were added by the peach and orchid floral detail — the former reflecting the pale walls of her room.

The outside background mingled five different browns which were very close in value. The inside background was given a little interest by closely blending two shades of tan in a mosaic effect.

The oversized rosebud in this design, so typical of the Aubusson, was Peach, with a small amount of Rose added to the dye solution. Considerable highlight was played up in its turned petals. The bell-like flowers were Orchid with a bit of Peach added to the dye solution. The other flowers were yellow and soft rusty golds. Most of the flowers blended out to almost white at the edges, or at the base of the petals. The foliage was Reseda and Bronze Green, to which a touch of Brown was added to develop the stems.

The shading from shadow to highlight in the sculptured scroll gives one the feeling that you can put your finger into the scroll and feel its concave effect. It was veined with Bronze Green. The turn-over of the knob at the beginning was extremely light beige, with a line of gold part way around the knob. It then blended from very dark brown shadows gradually into beige — then turned gradually darker into soft grayed Golds, Bronze, Bronze Green and dark values of Reseda, but using more of the latter where it branches off into the leafy detail. To make it turn over at its tip, very delicate shades of Reseda were used for highlights. Where it was necessary to save the dark Reseda tips of the scroll from the dark outer background, a few broken lines of the Rose and Peach were hooked at the edges.

It was one of the rugs shown at our earlier Exhibits — yet it made such an impression on me that I can see it very vividly, even to this day.

dominating flower colors from the center. This same development of shading may be applied to broad leaves.

10.   UNITY

You *gradually* determine all of the previous nine pertinent points as you hook your rug. Choosing your material and textures and deciding what is to be used for background and the largest areas of detail is a simple fundamental of starting your rug. Both problems are usually decided by the colors in the room where it is to be used.

All of the other important points come to your attention as you work. Ask yourself these questions as you hook:

Are my colors good neighbors, or good contrasts to each other?

Have I enough contrast of values in the varied details to give it interest?

Am I using my colors and values properly to maintain a good balance?

Have I carried every color I am using into some other detail so that this constant repetition gives continuity to my rug as a whole?

Have I been imaginative and inventive in my expression of color?

Have I used a little exaggeration to give added "oomph" to my detail?

If the answer is "Yes," then you have truly given your rug a feeling of UNITY.

A few may say: "I don't want to have to think of all these things when I hook a rug" and usually their rugs show it. But if you have read thus far you have just naturally absorbed some of the principles of color harmony. Given time to digest it, yes and perhaps re-read it, you will just naturally be more selective in your choice of color. You will do all this without being too conscious of the fact that you have become "choosy" about what you combine.

Others will say: "Oh, why didn't I learn more about color when I was younger? It would have helped me so much in the choice of colors within my home, and in the selection of my clothes." Then indeed has the study of color served one of its purposes — the increased enjoyment of its harmonious use. Truly, it makes the whole world look different!

Yes, hooking is going to be more fun now, for color has become so fascinating! I listened to a group of teachers recently chatting about their trip to New England in the Spring. One said: "I never really saw Spring before I studied color! Now its tiny bright green and rich red maple buds feathering the trees, its rich brown earth and the lovely contrast of white Shad growing in the woods was a new appreciation for me! Why there is beautiful coloring even in rocks! Yes, and that suit you are wearing, my dear, what a lovely background it will make!"

LOTUS

AN OVERTONE was given to "Lotus," hooked by Mrs. Nelson Read of Rockville, Conn., Emma Urban, Teacher, right from the dyepot. A mousy-brown background (a half teaspoon of Silver Gray to one pound of beige-gray material) was spotted with a mixture which contained something from all the motifs, as follows: one teaspoon Mulberry, one teaspoon Golden Brown, one teaspoon Myrtle Green, one teaspoon Bronze and two teaspoons Taupe. There was a slight variation in the values resulting, so that when hooked in straight lines lengthwise, it gave a jaspé effect to the background.

There were three combinations of colors prepared for the details of the design: #1 — five values from two parts Mulberry, one part Purple and one part Cherry; #2 — five values from two teaspoons Reseda Green over one pound of material; #3 — five values from four parts Medium Brown and one part Bronze. The secret of the overtone was in spotting each of these three after they were dyed with just a suggestion of the others.

The alternating petals of the plainer motif were developed in medium light to light blue-greens, with medium dark to medium blue-greens in the second petal, and the center of the first one was filled with the lighter golden browns, and the latter filled with a medium golden brown. The edge of the large circle was of the mulberries. The four petals extending from the center were developed of the greens at their centers; then browns in the middle area and the mulberries at the edge lying on the green background of the motif.

Now the same colors have been used in the alternate lacy motif, but with a quite different effect. Note how the dark values in the plainer motif are repeated in smaller details of this lacy motif. The petal-like extensions of this motif have an outer area of mulberry, an intermediate area of the browns and a center of green. Green is repeated for the scalloped area, upon which the petals repeat the same sequence of green center, brown intermediate area and mulberry edge.

Between the main motifs, the third smaller one is developed with a center of mulberry, identically the same as those in the other two motifs. The extending petals shade from green at the center to brown in the intermediate area, and are edged with the mulberry.

Thus a little of each dye solution was carried over into every other dye solution, even though in most instances it was just a mere tinge of color — giving the rug as a whole a beautiful overtone.

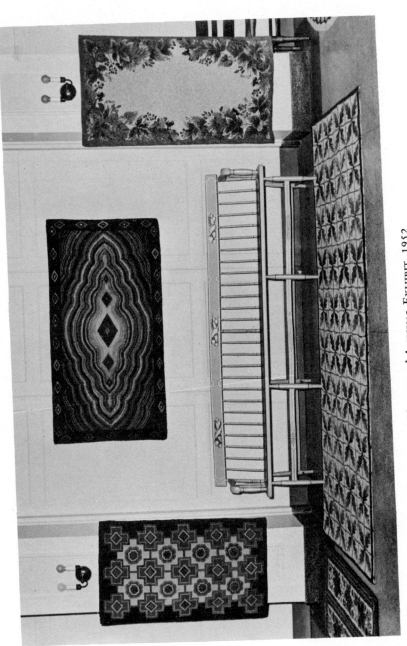

"OAK LEAVES" runner (before bench), hooked by Mrs. Joseph Tatro of West Boylston, Mass., Eva Bonci, Teacher, was made entirely from cast-off clothing — jackets, trousers, coats, etc. Some were simmered with a little detergent to become delicate tints of lavender, pink, blue, green or tannish tones. They were then given a common relationship through an extremely weak bath of Mummy Brown and hooked in little irregular "cobblestone" spots about the size of your thumb nail. The inch border and dividing lines were dull blue-green.

Varied gray garments and camel's hair tans were spotted with strong Purple, Strawberry, Plum, Cardinal, Mummy Brown, Bronze Green and Old Gold, in values to make four leaves in a block blend from dark base to light tip, each block of one general color.

It lies before a large fieldstone fireplace, in the hand polished pine-paneled living room of its creator.*

The center rug on the wall, "Eastland," was hooked by Mrs. Jessie Peterson Zehr, Teacher, of Oakland, Calif., Alice Brown, Teacher. In an analogous harmony of warm hues it repeats in rather subdued shades the general coloring of a beautiful antique quilt which dominated Mrs. Zehr's bedroom.

Dull Egyptian Reds were dyed of many values and intensities, to slide easily into paisley, which formed the main band of medallion. The bands inward changed to soft gold, rusty browns and light soft grayed greens. Outward, Mummy Browns blended with varied greens.

The center background was a very light beige. The diamonds repeated the paisley with brilliant intensities in outlines of greens.

"Vermont Geometric" (left), hooked by Mrs. W. A. Hunter, Stoneham, Mass., Harriet Snow, Teacher, combines seven shades of Old Rose with seven shades of Reseda for the square crosses and the circular motif, each one being spot-dyed with weak tints of the other. The outer background is Seal Brown and the inner background a tint of it over white.

The lightest part of a gray and white plaid blanket forms the background of "Woodland Sprite" (right) hooked by Mrs. Lee Grant of Detroit, Mich., Teacher. A gray tweed overcoat provided the outer background. Woodbine of Maroon, Wood Rose and Rose Pink, with berries of purplish-red; oak leaves of Maroon, Purple and Green, their acorns having brown bases and greenish-gold tops; hazelnut leaves of bright green with rosy tints, with nuts having green bases and gold tops provide colorful detail between the two backgrounds. The seed pods are a bright green with purple ruffles.

* Note: Antique bench by Mrs. Edith Cramer, Sutton, Mass., Author of "Handbook of Early American Decoration."

[171]

LEAF WREATH

MacKay Scroll

Many rugs are planned around family heirloom treasures. "Leaf Wreath," hooked by Mary Mitchell of Worcester, Mass., Teacher, began with her great great Grandmother's coverlet, woven in 1840. Its design had already inspired a hand-blocked drapery, in which the dull reds and midnight hues of the coverlet were imposed upon the creamy background of the draperies.

Later, Grandmother's lovely old blanket of a very faded red proved to be a perfect match for the red (R 5/12) of the coverlet, so it was used as the center background of "Leaf Wreath." The detail, therefore, had to be somewhat neutral. The large leaves were of midnight blue in plain and checked materials, and used again for the veins of the smaller leaves. Undyed neutrals, from dark gray to dirty white, were used for the sprays of smaller leaves.

Four rows of midnight blue were hooked at the edge of the rug. To make a soft transition between it and the red background, strips of bright red material were torn 12" to 15" long, and dyed this way: one-half teaspoon of Black and one-eighth teaspoon of Blue were mixed in one cup of boiling water. Very little of this was added to a plain dye bath, which covered one end of the strips held together with pinch clothespins. Gradually dye was added, and the material soused up and down to take on the desired gradation to hook it irregularly from center wreath to border, where the darkest value would blend into the midnight blue edge.

An old Paisley shawl helps to bind "MacKay Scroll," hooked by Gretchen W. Farr of New Smyrna Beach, Fla., Eleanor Aura Maxwell, Teacher, to a bedroom with creamy walls, gold theatrical gauze at the windows and maple furniture.

Cleverness was shown in the way the paisley had been fingered into a brown and goldish plaid for the darker values of the scroll, which were applied from the vein outward into highlights of soft gold and corny yellows, exaggerated at the tips of the side curls. As a dramatic contrast, the tawny yellows and soft golds on the other side of the mid-veins are fingered out into the plaid and paisley edges, most of which lie against the very dark mingled browns of the outer background. The inner background is a creamy blanket, slightly tinted with Mummy Brown. The roses in the corners and at the two ends of the center are keyed to the paisley colors through Maroon dye, while the others are a little lighter from Terra Cotta dye. The foliage of the corner roses is Olive Green on one side and Reseda on the other. Lessons had been interrupted, and Mrs. Farr had not been able to satisfy herself about the small leaves and stems in the center, but one day while in the woods, Eleanor Maxwell, in her quiet way, reached up and pulled off a small branch of a live oak tree, which had been broken and was quite dry, and said: "Here are the colors for the little leaves." It was perfect!

THIRTEEN STARS

BLUE HERON

THE COLOR plan of "Thirteen Stars," hooked by Mrs. Marguerite McCroskery of Stamford, Conn., Teacher, started with her son's khaki trousers and school uniform "blues," so the shades were on the faded side. The outer band was of the faded blue, the inner ground an off-white. The stars that lay upon the blue band were of greenish-gold (Bronze and Yellow), while the eagle and leaves repeated the greenish-gold, shadowed with the khaki trousers and darker values of Bright Green and Dark Brown dyes. The shield was of dull reds, white and the same faded blue of the outer band.

MR. WILLIAM M. CABOT, of the famous Cabot family of Boston, donated the greenish-blue smoking jacket which formed the bulk of the body of the "Blue Heron" hooked by Mrs. Ada Nealley of Hopedale, Mass., Marion H. Metcalf, Teacher. Greenish-blue predominated, with soft rose pinks playing a secondary part. The pond or swamp was created from old dresses dyed Turquoise Green and Aqua Green which were carried into the area between the two bands on the end. The darker shades were exactly like the formulas given for casserole dyeing in the Letter Service of May 15, 1942, thus utilizing a faded blue sport coat. These same dark shadows were used for the bulk of the lily leaves and for the background of the bands at both ends of the picture with circles of the color of the pool.

For contrast, the lilies in the pool were dyed with Rose Pink over white and cream for highlights, over light beige for medium tones, and over darker beige for shadows. The darker values of the Rose Pink were used for the lily and buds in the two borders, and for the lower horizon that formed a sunset. This horizon grows gradually lighter, and for that part which is lightest, where it meets the lightest value of the greenish-blues of the sky, a pink material had been treated with color remover to get a pinkish-gray. This made a perfect and an easy transition into the complement of delicate greenish-blue, which then gradually began to darken, and also strengthen, as it neared the top of the picture. The stronger greenish-blues were secured from Peacock over light gray.

The cat-o-nine-tails are of extremely dark brown, and their leaves a soft Bronze Green.

Miss Metcalf pays her pupil the compliment of following her suggestions faithfully, and adds that if all pupils would do likewise with their teachers, until they can use color harmoniously, more beautiful rugs would result. It's true!

NORMA ANTIQUE

BRIDAL RING

THE DETAIL in "Norma Antique," hooked by Mrs. Grace Pettee of Chelmsford, Mass., Mrs. Mary Boyd, Teacher, is somewhat small and sparse. Therefore, the value you apply to the background will turn it to a light, medium or dark rug, depending on what you use.

This background is a blend of two light beige materials, and by their directional lines of hooking give a mottled effect.

The flowers are, generally speaking, soft mahogany pinks, blending into Salmon highlights and Spice Brown shadows. Yet each flower has been given its own individuality by the use of more of one of these hues than the other. The flower centers are made interesting by the use of dark YGs, with single loops of Chartreuse pulled in among the darker values.

The large leaves of BG are veined and tipped with grayed Mahogany, which binds them to the flowers. Those in the corners are a bit more intensified. The long ferny sprays, which extend toward the center, are rather subdued in soft YGs, and veined with Spice Brown, a repetition from the flowers. Accents of BGs were used at the edges of many to tie them to the other foliage.

IN THIS "Bridal Ring," hooked by Mrs. John Haygood of Sunderland, Mass., Mrs. L. J. Cunningham, Teacher, an unusual dark background of blackish-plum (one part Silver Gray to two parts Plum over light gray) has been used under the double rings of the border, and underneath the floral bouquets in the center. A lighter, very grayed plum forms the rest of the background. It has been dyed irregularly so that in the hooking it takes on a very subtle mosaic pattern.

The two large inner rings and the smaller rings in the border are from several shades of Silver Gray, from lightest value on the outer edge to a medium dark inner circle.

Wine shadows blending into a combination of Wine and Cardinal (very soft shades), and highlights of tints of the same combination, with more Cardinal added, form the roses in two of the diagonal corners, and appears in its intensity in the two roses in the center. An extremely dark wine shadow at its base, or where one petal folds over another, and an extreme pinkish-white highlight on the edges of only three of its petals show the imagination and somewhat restraining hand of its creator. The white lilies reflect the silver grays of the rings in their shadows. The daisies which surround the bouquet are extremely soft with subdued shades of ecru and lavender. The whites are repeated again in the lilies-of-the-valley in the corners. All the foliage has been played down in extremely grayed shades of blue-greens and yellow-greens.

AGATHA ANTIQUE

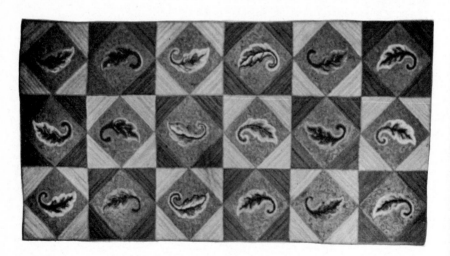

ANTIQUE LEAF

In "Agatha Antique," which is a copy of a treasured old needle-point rug, hooked by Mrs. E. N. Van Ornum of Los Angeles, California, Teacher, a delightful, rather subtle color harmony was secured from mahoganies and blue-greens of close values.

The general tone of the background is of mahogany browns, two dark brown materials having been given a Mahogany overcast by putting them through a Mahogany bath for the two slightly different borders. The corner background which has a cinnamon brown cast is Mahogany over medium beige, and the inner background of pinkish-beige is a tint of Mahogany over shell pink material.

The roses reflect the general tone of the various backgrounds, being of a brownish cast (Mahogany over light and medium beige). The small petaled flowers near them and in the corners are a deep pinky-brown, while the little flowers at the ends of the center bouquet are white with delicate pinks, blending into darker pink edges, just dark enough to keep them from being lost in the pinkish-beige background.

Complementary blue-greens are used in the foliage in a moderate soft intensity, with dark purple veins, the smaller off-shooting leafy detail being rather brighter greenish-blues. The little diamonds which lie upon the brownish oval border, emphasizing the medallion center, are outlined with bright pinky-brown, and filled with a light plaid material tinted Mahogany. The conventional motifs at ends and sides repeat the same blue-greens of the foliage.

"Antique Leaf," hooked by Mrs. Nelson Argueso of White Plains, N. Y., Katherine Eastman, Teacher, has been given a modern effect, not only by its low intensity of coloring, but by the directional lines of hooking. The background underneath all the leaves is the same, a slightly grayed greenish-blue. The corners of the blocks alternate. One square has light corners of light grays to white, and the next one has very dark corners of bluish-gray, which give it a checkerboard effect. It also produces the effect of having an intervening motif of diamonds with two extremely light pie-shaped pieces and two extremely dark pie-shaped pieces.

The leaves are in varied hues. Many blend from dark to light mahogany rose with green veins; some are of golds blending into green shadows with brown veins; some are rosy browns, blending into mahogany-red shadows with green veins; and some are bronzy green with brown veins, but they are all of very low intensity, so the entire rug is quite gray. Notice how some of the leaves shade from dark values along one side of the vein, out to light edges, and light values the other side of the vein to dark edges.

It made a lovely wedding gift!

LITTLE MIDDLEBORO

HEART'S DESIRE

DARK AND light contrasts are used in developing the scroll of "Little Middleboro" hooked by Edna Harrold, Teacher, of Napa, Calif., Alice Brown, Teacher. The scrolls are a grayed Bronze Green, spot-dyed with Mummy Brown and a little Turquoise Green. Every other scroll has a light grayed green turnover. The same colors are used in the outer border, with a light and medium line of the mulberry, repeated from the floral center. The background is a pinkish-beige (tint of Seal Brown and speck of Mahogany over old white materials). The lily is cream with tips slightly tinged with delicate pink, and has bronze veins and mulberry stamens. The two large flowers on either side are mulberry with green centers, freckled with deep mulberry. The daisies are white with gray shadows; the anemones spot-dyed blue and mulberry; and the lilies-of-the-valley a grayed blue.

DARK AND light contrasts are emphasized in the scrolls of "Heart's Desire," hooked by Mildred Wagner Hoos of Berlin, N. H., Marjorie Leggett, Teacher, which lies before a maple desk. Its background is Black (over medium gray, with a little Green added). Its scrolls are delightfully shaded from dark shadow to highlight, with ten different values of yellow-green, the darker ones dyed over medium gray, the medium shades over medium gray after the color was removed, and the lighter ones over a yellowish homespun blanket. The dyes were Dark Green, Yellow and Buttercup Yellow in varied strengths, in what she refers to as a "try and test method." The scrolls are veined with varied values of American Beauty dyed over medium gray and the homespun blanket, which are used again for the roses. The foxglove in five values of Copenhagen Blue over white, and two darker values of a deeper purple-blue undyed, repeats the blues of the draperies and a slip covered chair. The dahlias mirror the yellow highlights of the scroll. The sweet peas of pink (light values of the roses) and grape shades reflect the colors of a painting and a vase near by, and appear again in the padulas.

"HOT IRONS," hooked by Mrs. Harry Holmwood, Orchard Park, N. Y., Myra Schwarzmeier, Teacher, was made for a beloved daughter's home in Arizona. The design contains many well-known branding irons, which my readers may want to identify, as follows:

First Row (left to right)*

1. Horse Shoe
   E. C. King, Jr., Pittsburg, Tex.
2. Hat A
   E. J. Glynn, Del Rio, Tex.
3. Wagon Wheel
   T. H. Holland, Electra, Tex.
4. Flying TX
   Henry Greening, Crowell, Tex.
5. V Eight
   J. E. Baddus, Silsbee, Tex.

Second Row (left to right)

1. 4–5 Connected
   A. L. Casparis, Round Mt., Tex.
2. Bridle Bits
   Anton Elstner, Kerrville, Tex.
3. Cow Head
   Wm. A. Hardin, Ingram, Tex.
4. Boot
   Dan Stamp, Houston, Tex.
5. Cross Keys
   James D. Lynch, Waco, Tex.

Third Row (left to right)

1. Double R
   W. H. Rush, Middlewater, Tex.
2. Rolling W
   King Ranch, Kingsville, Tex.
3. Rising Sun
   B. E. Harris, Harris Valley, Tex.
4. Cross S
   W. A. Gilliam, Perryton, Tex.
5. Arrow Crescent
   Chas. E. Clamp, Brackettsville, Tex.

Fourth Row (left to right)

1. Longhorn Plus
   E. Coffee, Dora, Tex.
2. Double 7 Slash
   Jas. A. Sensing, Austin, Tex.
3. Dog Iron
   Will Rogers, Oklahoma
4. Clover Cross
   R. B. Coleman, Denton, Tex.
5. Twin Hearts
   J. M. Durst, Junction, Tex.

The background was a fine tan and white check. Actually the outline of the State of Texas appears within the diamonds in the pattern, but since this rug was to be used in Arizona, these diamonds were turned to a geometric motif.

Five shades of red, from two parts Egyptian Red and one part Mahogany, were used for two sides of the diamond, and five shades of Old Gold for the other two sides. The branding irons are three shades of the reds — dark, medium dark and medium — and are outlined with a dark Old Gold. Medium dark Seal Brown is used for the hexagon border, and the border at the edge of the rug.

Little boys, yes big boys too, will love this design!

*Illustration shows only second, third, and fourth rows.

UNITY

[184]

A DESIGN of varied motifs, like "Unity," hooked by Edna Fleming of North Easton, Mass., Teacher, must be properly balanced by color, to pull the units together as one.

In this type of design you can forget reality and use color as imaginatively as you wish. This one has a dark, rich mahogany background under the floral detail and in the border. A small gray and white mixture has been used to outline all the squares. Mahogany in three values form diagonal division lines in the alternating blocks.

A small plaid of grayed-blue and mahogany, plus plain and mixtured materials — two or three lines of one, and four or five of another — fill the area between the division lines and the half diamond, the latter being filled with the small plaid first used. In the opposite two the same materials have been repeated, but in different proportions, starting off with plain and darker grays, then using the mixtures and plaids from the other set, in various proportions, filling the half diamond with the same plain dark gray started with. Thus, viewed as a whole, the pie-shaped areas that form a frame around one block differ from those that form a frame around the intervening blocks, yet are of similar coloring.

The flowers are balanced by repetition of color. The rose of bluish-gray blends into soft greenish-gold edges of petals; the latter is repeated in the daffodils, and again as the sepals and stamens of the fuchsias, which have "skirts" and buds of the grayed-blue. Now, as you can see, that makes a triangular balance.

Light, very grayed blues form the petals of the morning glories, blending into dull mahogany throats, with a few accenting shadows of a very dull plum. The mahoganies are repeated in the dogwood. In their lighter values, they form the petals of the hibiscus. Dark plum shadows the light mahogany thumb prints at the base of their petals. The pistil is saved by being a rather bright chartreuse green filled with a lighter value. That gives another triangular balance.

The very grayed plums used for accents in these flowers are blended into grayed tints of mahogany for the iris. Delicate tints of both mahogany and plum merge into dark, dull, grayed plum shadows in the wild rose, with chartreuse accents in the stamens, and these two balance.

Thus, every flower has its own individuality, yet each repeats something from the others, so that the eye follows through and gives unity to the color plan as a whole.

WATSON SQUARE

MAZE BORDER

REPETITION is the keynote of "Watson Square," hooked by Marion L. Barrett of Cranston, R. I., Ellen H. Morton, Teacher. It was planned for her hall, and to tie up to her stair carpet of soft grayed myrtle green broadloom, and a beige wallpaper with pink mahogany figures. All sorts of white, beige, light and medium grays, light and medium tans, taupe, blue and gray checks were dyed in gradations of the two complements of Mahogany and Myrtle Green. Some of the greens were spotted with Mahogany, and some of the dull mahoganies were spotted with Myrtle Green, which gave an overtone to both. The whole rug was a repetition of these shades. A dark, dull mahogany outlined the border and dividing bands, which were filled with a slightly lighter mahogany spotted with Myrtle. The two smaller squares at each intersection were outlined with medium mahogany, while the space between was filled with spotted green, and the center square blended from dark mahogany at the outside edge into lighter values at the center. The diamonds had two outlines — a medium mahogany and a bright grape-like mahogany (Mahogany dyed over light blue), and filled with the odd shades of green, spotted with Mahogany. The background of bands and medallion was a light beige material "as is" (her daughter's coat).

The medallions were blended from dark values of Mahogany at outside edge, shading into lighter tones where they met the fingers. The fingers were of the Myrtle Greens, darkest at the edge and shading into slightly lighter values around the center. The little center was light at the outer edge, growing into darker shades in the middle.

IN THE "Maze Border," hooked by Mrs. Arnold Lehtola of Westminster, Mass., Mrs. Ralph S. Gavitt, Teacher, grays have been used for the two-toned background. Dark gray formed the background in the panels and the narrow border at the edge, while a lighter value of gray was used for the wider borders between.

The grapes were of rather striking purples and violets, the small berries of bright reds. Gay yellow-greens and blue-greens were blended in the varied leaf detail. The illustration shows how the lighter values lift the edges and tips of the leaves from the rather absorbing background. The acorns of brown blended into very light greens at their edges, where they met darker background.

In the maze of the borders, three lines of varied colors were carried for a short distance, and then blended into another set of three. In this way the maze constantly repeats all the colors from the center, thus binding it to the borders.

A STAIR runner may indicate the personality of the rugger. "Oak Leaves," hooked by Mrs. Vida Jopson of West Hartford, Conn., Teacher, shows vivacious and imaginative colors in the leaf detail. No effort is made to confine the colors to reality.

The background underneath the leaf detail is an extremely dark brown, with lines of soft red and brown where it meets the center. The inner background is of beiges and tans, with an occasional darker value of brown added, with consistent regularity, to give a uniform effect, thus distracting little attention from the glamorous leaf border.

The leaves are varied, some being bronzy-greens, some rusty and golden-browns, some rusty-reds and mahogany, some in soft peach to brown and an occasional one of turquoise blue. There is delightful repetition by making the veins of one leaf of the general tones of another, the turquoise is veined with mahogany, the red with brown, the browns with green, the greens with rust and the rust with turquoise.

The leaves are balanced from side to side by *values* of the different hues, rather than by the same hue. Thus, a particularly light leaf of soft peach to brown might be balanced by one of *similar values* in bronzy greens.

THE "ORIENTAL STAIR RUNNER," hooked by Mildred Yeaton of Shrewsbury, Mass., in Sally Newhall's class at Rose Cottage, was my experiment in applying several values of one hue in various ways, sometimes as an outline and sometimes as a filler, to give interest to a repeat pattern.

The center background and narrow edge were a dark, rich burgundy; the border background was a warm beige. A line of white separated the two.

All the motifs lying on the center background had three outlines of various mauves and tints of lavender blue and Burgundy. The rest of the motif was of soft grayed mauve, with inner cross of purple, edged with light lavender or pale blue, or of light lavender edged with purple. Each one varied slightly from its neighbor.

There were more variations in the border. Some of the squarish motifs were edged with white, pale blue and soft pink before being filled with dull old blue, with center square of mauve edged with gold. Others were of the same colors, but the filler of one became an outline in another. The vine was dull old blue edged with purple, with intervening motifs of blue with mauve centers edged with gold, but these, too, varied in the above manner. Those motifs directly opposite each other in the border were made the same for balance.

RUSTIC CHARM

[190]

REPEAT patterns should be developed in such a manner that all units are pulled together as one. This is achieved partly by overtones in dyeing and by repetition in applying the colors.

In "Rustic Charm," hooked by Mrs. Caleb Murdough of Baldwinville, N. Y., Adrienne Bradley, Teacher, all hues were given an overtone of Egyptian Red in the dyepot.

Green was used over medium grays for the darker outer background, and Green over light grays for the lighter background in the medallion.

Mixtures of Egyptian Red, Terra Cotta and Maroon were dyed in a range of values overdyed with onion skins and blended with varied colors in the colorful leaves in the medallions. Onion skin dyeing was combined with varied tan and brown materials "as is" for the pine cones and stem. The acorns were light tans at the top and mummy brown for the base.

In any detail in which natural materials did not have a weak wash of Egyptian Red, the overtone has been given by repetition of the hue.

By the way, nothing but old garments and blankets went into this rug.

"Rustic Charm" is the type of design men love, and Mrs. Murdough enjoyed making it for her husband's pine-paneled Study.

Applying Theory to Practice

It is assumed, when you start to hook a rug, that you are making it for a particular place in your home. Therefore, you have given some consideration to the type of design which would be suitable. The place where it is to lie will govern its dimensions, and the color scheme of the room will influence its coloring. Knowing that what you apply to the background (usually the largest area) will make it a dark, a light, a neutral or a colorful rug, according to your selection, you will be able to visualize it generally in its relationship to the room.

But you may interrupt me and say: "No, I am making this rug for my granddaughter as a wedding gift, and I don't even know what her home is to be like." But you have learned over a period of years that your granddaughter either has sentiment for the traditional or a preference for a contemporary design. You would know, too, of her taste in colorings. The best way is to have her choose the design and discuss the general coloring which she would like.

But do I hear someone say: "Now, wait a minute. I am hooking because I love to hook, and I am going to sell my rug. How can I be sure my rug will find a ready market?" Until you find special customers who want particular types of rugs, choose those designs suitable for the average home of today. "Pelham Diamond," "Wedgewood," "Mooney Pansy," "Romantique" or "Fascination" are good examples.

But I can even hear some say: "Mine are not for my home, and are not for anyone in particular. I just love to hook." Well, then, put your hours of work into your rugs and suit your *own* fancy. The joy of the work itself will have served its purpose in providing a method of expressing yourself in color. Your family will love them because you made them, and even if there is no family to enjoy them, creating rugs is like putting money into the bank — sometime their value can be withdrawn.

So let's get down to applying theory to practice, no matter why you are hooking.

First, choose the colors that will be like those in your room — or those that will please the recipient of your gift — or those which will fit an average home. In the latter case, avoid unusual and exotic colorings.

Now identify their general position on the Color Wheel. It may be they all lie in one general hue, but if there is more than one hue (and there usually is), you may discover they automatically fall within a definite color harmony. This is an assurance that they will develop well together. Having chosen which color is to be the most intense, draw a rough circle and check the colors included. Then draw a line inward from the most intense color you will use, to serve as a reminder that the other hues will be in varying degrees of intensity.

Now let's look at the Dye Wheel, and see what dyes lie within the area of the colors you intend to use. Remember, you are not limited to any one dye. You can add a small amount of any neighbor to pep up a hue, without losing its identity, and thereby get lovely "off-colors," which may tie it to your room more closely. From the various dyes and countless combinations of those lying within the area of these hues, you are unlimited in what you can create. It is fascinating to experiment with them! When dyeing, you will, of course, use less dye of all the hues (in varying degrees) than the one which is to be most intense.

Review "Dyeing for Backgrounds," and the section on this subject under "Ten Pertinent Points," because there you will find many practical suggestions for this all-important part of your rug and can make your choice from all the different values and intensities of your chosen colors. Be sure it is related to your color plan. If using several colors in a floral bouquet, keep the inner background grayed or neutral. I once heard Mary Mitchell, Teacher, say: "When using color in floral detail, choose at least an inner background that could not be identified as a specific color."

When dyeing for flowers, keep the diagonal path in mind, getting dark, rich values up to light, weak tints, or vice versa, dark, dull values up to light, bright ones. They will be more alluring than the vertical path of straight gradation. Lay them over your finger so only about one-eighth inch of each will show, one against the other, and cover the top one with your right hand, so you will see only a small amount of highlight, for that is the proportion in which they will be used. Of course, if the color plan calls for the simplicity of contemporary style, the vertical gradation will be better.

Now in selecting color (or dyeing) for foliage, remember it serves to bring out the beauty of the flowers, and usually plays second fiddle in importance, so its intensity should be somewhat duller. Depending upon the colors that come within your plan, look beyond the usual BG, G and YG for leaf materials. You can use Bronze or Khaki Drab, or, depending upon the design, even go into some of the brown dyes for foliage. It might be necessary to add a small amount of weak yellow-green dye to pull them together with others. You can go beyond BG to weak B, or even PB for some shadowy leaves. Swinging into the neutral pole though, and using the grayer shades, is much safer.

In dyeing for scrolls, choose a color which will be related to one of the colors in your plan — either the flowers, foliage or background. If it is a large scroll, covering quite an area, keep the intensity down, relying upon strong color, if wanted, for very small areas or accents. Be sure to get a wide variety of values. You will need some very dark values for emphasis. How about some small plaids, checks or mixtures for those darker values, to intrigue the eye? Several values, gradually growing lighter, will give the scrolls more contour. You will probably need much more of the intermediate values and lower intensities than of the shadows and the highlights. Hold them over your finger, too, to see how they grade up from dark to light, and this will give you the general effect of how they will look when hooked. Almost immediately you will see what is lacking, or what is out of line, either in value or intensity.

If your scroll covers a wide area, watch your intensities. It may be colorful without being garish. It is usually the intermediate shades which fill the greater part of the body of the scroll, and these shades determine the general effect you will achieve. Use your intensity, if you want it colorful, but watch your proportions. Sometimes you will want to make the scroll more important than the floral center, in which case your values will be widely contrasted. At other times you will want to sink the scroll into the background, in which case your values will be close.

Get contrast into your flowers, too. Even when there are several flowers alike of one hue, one may have more dark values, another more medium values and others much more of the lighter values. Where there are several different flowers, each flower may be a contrast in value as well as of color, from the others. For example, a rose may be of very dark values of R, a tulip of medium values of P, and petunias of the very lightest value of B. When in doubt as to what color to use in any flower, you are always safe in making it white, with colorful accents, of course, to bind it to the others. The contrast of values in the various details delights the eye! It is always best to get a small area of background hooked near the detail as you work, for it is a warning to you when the value at the edge of your flower or foliage gets too near the value of your background (especially if the two are of the same general intensity), for then you are apt to lose it.

Shadow those leaves when they run in under a flower, which will give depth, but watch the contrast of value where this detail meets the background. If you use a very dark, rich shadow on a leaf that lies on a very light background, it will probably be too dramatic, both in value and intensity. In that

[195]

QUAKER (A PAIR)

A VARIATION of values in "Quaker," hooked by Lillian Knight of Worcester, Mass., member of Hookrafter's Guild, gave additional interest by using more of the dark values in one rose, and more of the lighter ones in others. Deep, rich shadows to delicate highlights came from varied mixtures of Rose and Mahogany, Maroon and Old Rose (the latter two over white), Woodrose over pink, and Maroon, American Beauty and Cardinal over pinks and beiges. In the center, for instance, the smallest rose was of darker values, another one from dark to medium with only a small amount of highlight, while a third had only a small amount of dark and intermediate values blending into much lighter highlights. You will note the corner roses were developed in a similar manner. The tulips changed slightly from the hue of the rose by using dark Burgundy and Plum for the shadows, blending into rather grayed old rose shades at the tips. The little five-petaled flowers introduced a second color, a soft old blue.

All the leaf foliage of varied blue-greens has been played down somewhat into the background, with formulas taken from Dye Dabbler #58. Their veining is of light or dark greens, or of the grayed shades from the roses.

The background of five values of Taupe and Mahogany over white and light gray has a halo effect, shading from medium dark warm Taupe at the edge, gradually lightening to a light area around the floral center, then growing gradually darker into shadowy tones (darker than the edge) underneath the floral center.

THE BACKGROUND in this "Quaker," hooked by Mrs. Adelaide Miller of Kansas City, Mo., Mrs. Margaret Hunt, Teacher, is two parts Ecru, one part Taupe over medium dark gray.

The delicate roses of Ecru have white highlights, and blend into dusty rose and Mahogany centers. The tulips blend from dark values of Mahogany dye at the edges, into lighter dusty pink, and are then fingered into delicate aqua at their base. The little white flowers are shadowed with Ecru and a medium dusty rose for greater emphasis, with soft gold centers. Thus the deeper shades in all these flowers were either nearer the outer area of the floral center at the edges of the tulip petals, or at the center of the roses.

The rosebuds had more intensity of color, and some seemed to combine the hues of both tulips and roses. The leaf foliage was delightful, being extremely subdued, and sinking away somewhat into the background. Very grayed Bronze Green was used for those, shading into light tips, some of which were two delicate tints of pink from the roses. Some of them were veined with Mahogany and dusty pink, and others of darker values of the leaves. An occasional pale leaf was made of a very soft grayed green. A consistent repetition of the same development of each little cluster of four leaves, which appears so often in this design, gave unity.

case, dark, *dull* shadows would be better, and a line or two of the lighter values on the edge of the leaf where it lies against the light background will make the contrast less severe.

Watch your balance; study the design and see how many flowers of one kind are in opposite directions, either across, or diagonally, or in triangular positions. Then, if they are made generally the same, you seldom have a balance problem. Little knobby ends in scrolls may also turn lighter or darker, and if there are several of these, you can balance them in opposite or triangular positions, too.

Repeat your colors from one flower or floral detail to another, and remember, no matter how small the repetition, you are unconsciously aware of it. Your dark red roses, for instance, may have blackish brown shadowy accents (if you are working on the warm side and using rust and goldish shades), or even blackish-green from the leaves, or the neutral blacks. This accent does not necessarily have to be large. Only two or three loops pulled in three or four places, where the shadows would be the darkest, will give repetition.

Or, if they swing slightly toward RP–R, blackish-purple shadows in a dark red rose may be carried forward from a purple tulip, or even navy from a light blue pansy. Watch for other ways of introducing touches from other flowers, like the edges of petals, the "whiskers" of a pansy, the throat of a morning glory, the stamens of a lily or the centers of flowers.

Different types of leaves can take on a definite BG, G or YG cast, but blending one into the other, either through dye or when hooking, will give more unity. Thus a small amount of the shadows of a blue-green leaf can be carried over into the shadows of a yellow-green leaf. The highlights of a yellow-green leaf can be brought over as tips in a blue-green leaf.

The same principles of repetition are true in developing fruit designs. You can always give repetition to fruit, by carrying forward even a lighter value to some other fruit. Thus, lighter shades of a red apple could be carried forward into the blush of a pear; the soft grayed shades of a purple plum could be carried forward into the blush of a peach.

In most scrolls, which usually form a border for a design, you must keep a feeling of continuity. Don't jump from dark values in one section into extremely light values in the next. Slide from one into another gradually, so the eye easily follows from very dark to light. Otherwise, it may become disjointed. If your plan is to combine one or more hues in your scroll, use close values, that is, the same value of blue, for instance, as of green (and of the same intensity), where you change from one to the other, to keep continuity. If the colors are not neighbors, the introduction of just a bit of the color you are skipping will help to make a smoother transition. Thus a blue-green in a scroll, which you wish to turn to gold accents, will slide easier into the gold if you introduce just a little of the intervening G and YG between the two. Spot-dyed material is a wonderful help in making these transitions.

Imagination is a priceless gift which has been given to you, if you will but use it. Oh, I know you say you haven't got it, many people do, but, given encouragement, they have more than they realize, and giving vent to it is such fun! You will surprise even yourself! Try it on some ferny leaves; repeat your varied greens, making each pinnate slightly different. Pull in an occasional exaggerated tip of a pale tint of one of the flower colors. Oh, you'll have a lot of fun with these!

Exaggerate, yes, embroider your detail a bit. Ruth Higgins calls it "Titivating." It's a good word. It can often be done best just before completion. Stand off and get the distant view. Squint your eyes. If something stands out like a sore thumb, now is the time to push it back. Dull it down. Look for those intense loops that make it do that, and replace them with slightly softer tones nearer the neutral pole, and the whole thing will take its proper place. Now look again. Is something lost? Well, let's glamorize it with a bit more intensity. Let's pull in *this* very gay scarlet at the fluted edge of the tiny "cup" in the white narcissus. "That," you say, "How dare you"? But it's only going to be a few loops and when they are in,

OPEN FLOWER

WINTER SUNSET

REPETITION of both flower and foliage colors from the center to the border bound the two together in "Open Flower," hooked by Mrs. Wilhelmina Gustafson of West Hartford, Conn., Elizabeth A. McCabe and Lillian Kennedy, Teachers.

The flowers are in various intensities of Terra Cotta with very dark accents at base, and appear quite peppy lying against a background of light rosy beige that has a slightly mottled effect. The leaves are in various blue-greens, mostly Myrtle Green, and are veined in lighter values of leaf or floral hues.

The blocks in the border are outlined with dark brown, and are alternately developed of the flower and leaf shades, from very dark to very light values. They also alternate in the two rows, so that the flower shades on the outside row are opposite the leaf shades on the inside row.

REPETITION is just as important in pictorials as in rugs. In "Winter Sunset," hooked by Esther Mann of Oakham, Mass., Gladys Skiffington, Teacher, all sorts of tweedy mixtures are used again and again. Brown and tan tweeds form the border, and are carried over into other detail. Gray, green and brown tweeds are in the trunks of the dark, dull blue-green trees in the distance. Livelier blue-greens are used for the trees in the foreground, and for the river, which darkens at the edges against the snow. Slightly lighter and brighter blue-greens, as well as yellow-greens, are used to lighten and lift one bough from the other in many of the trees.

The snow capped mountains are tinged with peachy reflections of the setting sun, and with dark purple-blue shadows near their base. The setting sun brings warmth to the scene. Its deep crimsons and salmons, mixed with light yellows over the top, soften where it meets the delicate peach sky. Their intensities are carried forward into the river as reflections. Grays and taupes form the clouds, which are also tinged with reflections from the sun. The long shadows cast by the setting sun are of taupe against varied whites of the snow.

their intensity will be lost somewhat against the other softer colors. "Well, who would have believed those few loops would pick it up so well?"

Look at it again. Does it lack a variation of values? How about making the stamens in those light lilies a much darker value? What about blending those white flowers into tints of an important color? How about using lighter values at the edges of three out of five of the petals on those smaller flowers?

What about more dark values? How about a few lines of *very* dark purple blending into lighter and softer violets, as colorful accents in the base of that golden tulip?

Do your white flowers look too "blah"? Perhaps your white roses seem flat. Give them a colorful center, a repetition from one of your flowers. Of course, you would first have to use a tint of it before strengthening the color, or the jump from a neutral white to an intensity of color would be too sudden. Combine imagination with exaggeration! This might be your chance to pull the delicate suggestions of a purple tulip, a pink rose and a gold lily into the edges of the outer or inner petals of a white rose. Rank exaggeration, you say? Have you ever studied the colorful edges of a Peace Rose? Besides, it's a heap of fun to *dare* to exaggerate!

But someone interrupts: "But wait a minute. I'm not working on a scroll or floral, I'm making a geometric. A geometric always puzzles me. I never can quite see the possibilities of color in its simple lines. How do I start?"

Well, the same principles apply. You can use any color plan in a geometric, just as you can in any other type of design. Let one hue lead the others. Use it in the larger areas in its grayer shades, and in stronger intensities in its smallest areas. If it is to have two or more hues, let the second one be of less importance, and if a third is used, of much less importance.

Background now becomes broken up into smaller areas, but, as a rule, whatever you apply to these background areas, they will still cover a greater part of your design. Thus, what you apply to them will make your rug of that particular color.

The values, though, may vary. You can still maintain an all-over effect by two different values of one hue, as in "Fletcher Geometric," illustrated herein. If you apply two different colors, though, you may attract too much attention, unless they are extremely grayed. In such a case, two neighboring hues would be best because they would flow together.

Texture is very important in this geometric you are to make, for it is the mixtured materials that do something to the different areas of your pattern that make it so intriguing.

A number of values are better than a few, even though some are used infrequently. Slight contrast of values in the greater area of the pattern is subtle, but you still need a little of the extreme contrast of values in some of the detail for interest. An exception might be one in which you are developing a contemporary color plan, where color is not important and the contrast of values is close. When using pastels, it is better to avoid the limitation of light values. They have an insipid effect. It really requires some darker values and a small amount of stronger colors to give them character.

If a design has an alternate block like "Unity," the balance of the small size could be secured in the triangular manner, as shown in (1), and in the larger size, as shown in (2).

A		B
	C	
B		A
	C	
A		B

(1)

A		B		A
	C		D	
B		A		B
	D		C	
A		B		A
	C		D	
B		A		B
	D		C	
A		B		A

(2)

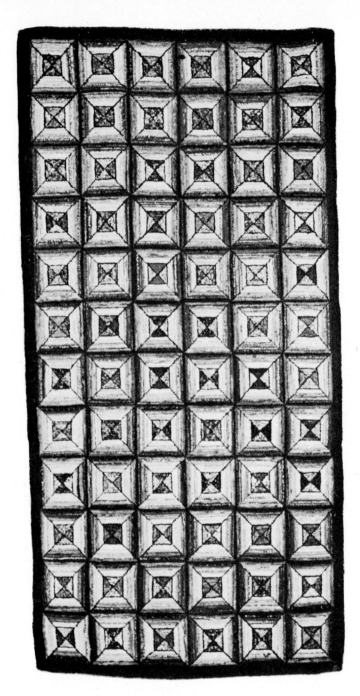

STAINED GLASS WINDOW

[204]

"STAINED GLASS WINDOW" was hooked by Mrs. Harriet Beaver of Sharon, Mass., Verna McCrillis, Teacher. What could be more appropriate with her lovely antiques than geometrics in which soft greens and wood rose shades predominated! The illustration shows clearly the variation of textures of checks and plaids.

A range of Reseda Greens was dyed, and the darkest used to square off the block and make the outside border. Others were combined with a few streaks of yellow-green, plus a few tweeds and plaids, for two sides of a square.

For the other two sides, several values of Wood Rose were dyed and blended, from dark edge at the outside of the square, to lighter values within, turning to beige tweeds and mixtures around the small center square. The blocks alternate, so the greens appear at the top and bottom of one, and at the sides of the next one, etc.

All sorts of dark valued plaids, having either rose or green dominating, were used as fillers for the little center windows. No two were exactly alike, yet they were all of a similar value, and their darker values were a contrast to the lighter wood rose and green shades lying next to them.

Great discrimination was shown in the choice of all sorts of plaids and mixtures, and by their application to the areas of the design to create harmony of color and a pleasing quiet effect in the way they were mingled.

If this design you are working on develops a secondary motif, like "Antique Leaf," where the corners of the squares will form diamonds between the leaves, some consideration must be given to what is going to happen when you apply colors to these areas. They should be of secondary importance color-wise. The principles of applying color to geometrics have been pretty thoroughly discussed in my pamphlet, "The Gist of Geometrics."

In all geometrics use repetition as much as possible. The general color of the main motif may be repeated as a filler in another. It is permissible, and sometimes desirable, especially in the larger geometric rugs, to improvise with slightly different values of a color in the different motifs, and sometimes even with color itself, if within the general color plan, so all the figures are not too exactly alike. I am always glad to hear that a person has run short of a certain color when working on this type of design because then she has to improvise with something similar, and often arrives at a much more interesting effect. It is the surprise element that attracts the eye! Therefore, when you start to gather the materials for your geometric, put those of the same general value and intensity together, even though they vary slightly, and use first one and then another in single lines of accents in a motif, and see what delightful changes it makes in the pattern.

You give continuity to your pattern by a consistent repetition of one general hue in the main outlines of a motif throughout the whole rug. Your second important hue for the secondary motif will add to this continuity, but always bind them together, using something of one in the other. In developing the main motif, it is not necessary to blend your color in a strict gradation of values, vertically, diagonally or horizontally. You can develop the frame of a motif in two hues, as an example, a frame of a deep yellow-green may gradually grow lighter and end up with two or three lines of two lighter values of bronze of similar intensity.

When you play one color against another in geometrics or conventionals you get very different effects than in floral designs. Playing some hues against others will produce a certain vibrancy. For instance, a rather bright blue against a rather bright green will give you a vibrant blue-green that has more snap and pep than a material changed with blue-green dye.

If you are going to use complementary colors in this geometric, and you hook one against another in the frame of a motif, it will make each of them appear brighter. If you find they are too bright and you want to dull them down, replace a line or two with a grayed tint of the richer color next to it and it will wash out some of the intensity.

The real charm of a geometric is in its contrast of texture, color and values, bound together by repetition to give it continuity. But do not let it become confusing to the eye by dramatic contrast of color used in a spotty manner, or the rug will not be easy to live with.

Exaggerate in geometrics by repeating something of importance in intensity in small areas, which gives jewel-like flashes of color.

Did I hear some one say: "But mine is an Oriental?" I have already covered this subject fairly well in my pamphlet, "The Objectives in Orientals," but will refer to them again briefly, from the color angle. Many desire to use the colors widely separated from each other on the Color Wheel, such as rich reds, blues and golds, often seen in Orientals of angular lines. Let your balance be uneven, use more reds, or more blues, for instance, than the other two. Confine the intensity to one of the three, and use it in small areas for the outlines or small fillers, but it may be repeated in other values, and lower intensities, in various other parts of the pattern. The larger the area, the darker and richer the color may be, or the lighter and softer. Your colors will have a closer relationship if you add just a bit of one dye to another. Of course, the important thing, as a rule, is to make that rug fit into your room, and if

KEY BORDER ORIENTAL

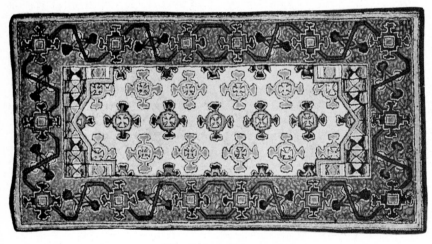

WORCESTER ORIENTAL

Reds and blues dominate in this "Key Border Oriental" hooked by Sylvia Spencer of Greenfield, Mass., Teacher.

Dark values of a lively navy appear in the large areas of the background around the center motif and outside border. Two different values of lighter blues were secured from a mixture of Copenhagen Blue and a little Peacock over cream and white, and used for the background of the alternating bands of the spandrels, and again in the outer part of the center motif which is bordered with gold and dirty white. It is also used as a filler for the alternating keys in the wide border, which lie upon an off-white background. Small amounts were again used to flank the gold and white division lines between the blue bands in the spandrels, and for either outline or filler in the tiny detail of the smallest motifs around the center.

Varied red flannels and violent shocking pinks were all put through enough Egyptian Red dye to bring down their intensities. These were used in the large area of background between the spandrels and the center medallion — in the dark detail of the center motif — the alternating keys of the wide border — and combined with paisley in the wavy bands that lie upon the alternating blue bands in the spandrels.

The small motifs of the center medallion and the narrow barber striped border are developed from the blues, reds, paisley, golds and white, with a very tiny bit of jewel-like bright green.

This "Worcester Oriental," hooked by Mr. Ralph Smith of Charlton, Mass., Mrs. Ralph Smith, Teacher, is a type of design that men enjoy hooking. After he had planned a small section of each border and one fourth of the center panel, his color problems were over and he was ready to make progress.

The key color, a luscious Oriental red, of slightly varying values, is in the background of the wide border. It was scarlet material, softened with a bit of Reseda Green and darkened with spotty Maroon. The squares within are outlined with deep beige, navy and light greenish-gold, and filled with medium light old blue.

The little intervening motif is outlined with navy and greenish-gold, and the knobby ends are filled with medium old blue, changing to a light green where it extends in to form a diamond. The center diamond is outlined with beige, dark maroon, and filled with greenish-gold. The band which runs between these motifs and gives continuity to the border is outlined with navy and filled with medium old blue.

The background of the center is deep beige. The center motifs are of old blues, outlined with navy and greenish-gold, and filled with darker blues at the extremities and lighter blues around center. The inner cross is outlined with navy, and filled with the varied reds. The end sections repeat the same colors. He loves it in his pine-paneled hall!

other Orientals are used there, you should pick up the same general coloring and use one hue in greater proportion than the others.

Of late, more and more people have become interested in the Persian Orientals, which have the curving lines and the conventionalized flowers. In these, the colors may be softer and include most of the floral tones. As an example, I worked out one for the Dye Dabbler #65 and #66 covering "Omár Kháyyám," in which a complementary harmony of B and YRs were used for the greater area, but a small amount of neighboring hues of R and PB were added. The same principles could be applied to any set of complements and their neighbors. Back issues of these Dye Dabblers are always available.

Now you have finished your rug. Let's give it a final look.

Does one hue lead in intensity? Are the others nearer the neutral pole?

Has it some interesting textured detail?

Is there a definite relationship between the background and detail?

Are the larger areas subdued to the brighter detail or, contrariwise, if the larger areas are somewhat colorful, are the details played down in low intensities?

Has it some dark and some light values? Has it some weak and some bright intensities in a pleasing combination? The proportions may be widely varied, but they should all be there in some part.

Is the eye satisfied with the balance?

Look for your repetition of color, from one unit or detail to another. Can you see them, or do you feel conscious of them?

Have you dared to exaggerate?

Then you have given it UNITY. You have created something you can be proud of. There is no thrill like it!

Or perhaps you are not yet quite satisfied. While you have worked, other ideas have come into your mind. This rug is finished, but already you are looking forward to using new ideas on your next rug.

For if you keep your mind open, you will find a constant flood of new ideas waiting to be used.

Yes, this rug is good, in fact everyone loves it! But right now you are raring to go on the next one, which you are sure will be the *best one yet!*

HILL'S LEAVES

WILD ROSE LATTICE

"HILL'S LEAVES," hooked by Mrs. Helen Hill of Littleton, Mass., Mrs. Royal C. Hope, Teacher, chose this design because of its name and followed the Dye Dabbler for its color plan. The large sprays of leaves at the ends blend from soft brick reds to delicate mahogany shades. The second sprays are Olive Green, shading into a delicate sage green, and the third sprays are a brownish-gold, blending into a delicate corn yellow. The main color of each of these sprays is carried over to its neighbor through repetition of shadow or highlights, to bind the three together. The inner band is a blend of the three hues, and the background is a light greenish-gray. The instructions stress the use of mixed materials, such as herringbones, tweeds, checks and rather colorless plaids in dyeing the colors called for, in order to give texture to this simple design. Mrs. Hill, who came into class more interested in learning how to braid, was soon fascinated with hooking and became an enthusiastic rugger, after having finished this rug.

IN A DESIGN like "Wild Rose Lattice," hooked by Mrs. William Hajdukiewicz of Gardner, Mass., Mrs. Ralph S. Gavitt, Teacher, the lattice detail is played down, serving merely to break up an otherwise plain background. Its treatment of color, therefore, is subtle, being a value only slightly darker than the beige background, and the lines are dropped casually where they meet the detail. The outer background is navy, complement of the beige inner background.

Some of the wild roses are in varied values and intensities of Rose dye; others are secured from Strawberry dye; in a few the two are "married," by combining both in one flower. Burgundy and Wine dyes provide the shadows in all of them, and thus bring them into a common relationship.

Most of the leaves are in varied yellow-greens, much of it being dyed over tweeds. A few of the leaves introduce blue-greens.

RAGS TO RICHES

SOMETIMES there are limitations to the colors you may use, because of personal dislikes as was the case in "Rags to Riches" hooked by Mrs. Lee Bird of Upton, Mass., Mrs. Eleanor Loftus, Teacher. Mrs. Bird's husband, being a Doctor, had seen too many green walls in hospitals, and requested that reds be used in the background of the rug she was making for his Study. Since the greater area of this design is background, it seemed a ticklish job to develop it of reds. However, many values of dull reds were secured from Mulberry and Maroon dyes, and deepened and dulled with a little Black for the area under the floral bouquets. Lighter grays of varied values were dyed with weaker solutions of the same dyes, and these were applied to the small all-over diamond background, shading them from dark edges to a light, soft grayed tint at their centers, thus repeating the effect of the diamond-leaded windows in the Doctor's Study.

The roses were of brighter intensities of the same Mulberry and Maroon dyes. The very soft grayed purplish-blue morning glories (Copenhagen Blue dulled with Taupe) blended into white throats and funnels. An interesting note is the white tulip, copied from an old fabric, with shadows of Khaki Drab and dull Gold. Additional contour was given them in the flare of the petals by the directional line of hooking of both shadow and highlight.

The large flat padulas of taupy-gray had grayed Mulberry edges to their petals, shading down into creamy bases, and the Mulberry was repeated in the center stamens. The other four-petaled "padula" is cream on the plain side of the petal, a little darker value of the cream on the other side of the petal, with grayed Mulberry veining.

All the leaves are of varied blue-greens with accents of yellow or brownish-green, particularly in the larger rose leaves.

The flowers in the corner diamonds repeat the same general colors of the center.

In her part of the program of the Teachers' Conference, preceding the Teachers 1953 Annual Exhibit, Mrs. Loftus said: "The invitation to be inventive is probably the most generous gift Color has to offer."

AGAMENTICUS

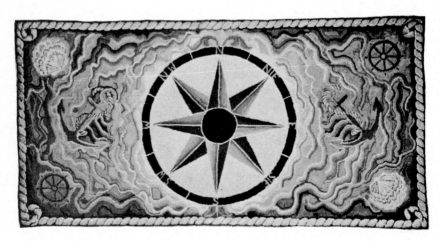

NORTH STAR AND COMPASS

THE BACKGROUNDS of rugs that lean toward the Early American or primitive designs are usually done in a manner of that period. Thus "Agamenticus," hooked by Mrs. May Harwood of Syracuse, N. Y., Adrienne Bradley, Teacher, has given a swirling, directional move to the inner background, which somewhat follows the lines of the scroll. For this, an old cream blanket was dyed (and probably crowded) into a bath of Old Ivory, which gave it slightly different values.

The flowing scroll is of many different values and moderate intensities of Egyptian Red and Terra Cotta dyes, darker in the outer areas, shading slightly lighter and repeating this before softening to the lighter values along the inner side. Notice there is considerable irregularity to the swirling lines of the scroll, shown by the shading, which is encouraged by the lines of the design.

The hue of the scroll is carried into the roses of the center, and is played against yellow-green leaves (Olive Green and Myrtle Green dyes), veined with the hue of the roses. All of the buds are lighter values and softer intensities, so they sink somewhat into the background.

THE BACKGROUND of "North Star and Compass," hooked by Mrs. Frances Hunt of Hanson, Mass., Margaret Farnsworth, Teacher, is made of all sorts of blues, "as is," several lines of each one being hooked in a directional line to give it a swirling, motion-like effect. It grows lighter around the center compass and darker at the corners.

The main point of interest is the compass, which has a dark blue band (outlined in gold), in which the various directions are noted, and a soft, warm, beige-tan background around the star center. The star, having an outline of gold, is of red on one side of each point and bright navy blue on the other side. A line of gold runs around the center circle which is filled in with the navy blue.

The other motifs are of much less importance. The shells are made of delicate opalescent pinks, with darker values giving them a fluted effect, and the wheels of dark Mahogany. The anchors on either side of the compass are purple-grays, with rope of the same grayed shades with a glint of gold that forms the border.

L'Faughnan

VARIATIONS of the general values may be given to flowers of the same kind, if you are careful to balance them. Thus, in this "L'Faughnan," hooked by Mrs. John J. Fahey of Wellesley, Mass., Mrs. John H. Stewart, Teacher, the roses at the right of the lower center border balance those at the left of the upper center, while the other two, diagonally opposite, balance in slightly grayer shades. The large flat padula-like flowers balance by using more dark values on those on the two ends, and quite light values on those at the center side.

Mrs. Fahey uses almost no material "as is," except possibly for background, but dyes just about everything. She believes, too, that "bleeding" new materials softens them. As an example, all the roses are from "bleeding" a maroon flannel skirt — tearing it up first into strips, and taking the strips from the pan at intervals — that gives her many values, up to her lightest desired tints.

The tulips at the ends are gold, blending into bluish edges, the other two in grayed-lavenders, with darker values to indicate the throats.

The large flat padulas are made from a blue flannel bathrobe, first bled to the desired values, and then spot-dyed with Lavender, Maroon and Rose.

The little flowers are made from a pastel (almost white) plaid skirt, but she added tints of pink or lavender or green or yellow, depending upon which hue the white flower should lean toward, so there is a delightful variation in all of them.

The leaves around the roses are blue-greens, and those around the tulips yellow-greens, while many of them are spot-dyed with the varied hues of the flowers.

The outer background is a very dark maroon, carried under the floral band. The inner background is beige — a spring coat of her daughter's.

ENTICE

RATHER close values of one color have been applied to "Entice" hooked by Mrs. Lauretta M. Southworth of Fall River, Mass., Evelyn A. Cloutier, Teacher.

Its background combines tints of Taupe with a little Cardinal for the inside, and two values darker for the outside.

The scrolls, made from several values of Mahogany, with a tint of Cardinal, sink away somewhat into the background in the outer area, because its light values are very similar to the value of the outer background. Its veins are exaggerated.

The roses repeat the scroll colors. A variation of values from Plum and Purple dye were given a weak wash of the scroll colors to bind them to the roses and then applied to the tulips. Tints of Navy in the morning glories blend down into darker values, and thence into deep purple throats (a repetition from the tulips). The fuchsias combine light purples in their sepals, and tints of the mahogany and cardinal in their "skirts," thus repeating colors from both tulips and roses. Because their values are very near the value of the background, they have a delicate wispy effect. The same is true of the tiny bud-like flowers that feather the outer area of the bouquet, which are a combination of Chartreuse and Old Gold tints.

The foliage is of varied yellow-greens (Olive Green), the rose leaves being dyed over tweeds and checks.

MILLER FLORAL

Who would believe that all the lovely floral detail in "Miller Floral," hooked by Mrs. Donald G. Humphrey of Toledo, Ohio, Mrs. Robert D. Franklin, Teacher, was once old garments?

The background of this rug is a delicate grayed pink (a tint of Wine in five values over tan and plaid blankets) forming a light halo around the floral center. The background under the flowered center is delicately shadowed with four shades of Plum over the same material. This reflected the tones of the walls in the room where it is to be used.

The roses are more intense than the other flowers (being equal parts of Strawberry and Aqua Wine over tan, gray and white). The rosebuds and rose hips are of the same hues.

The blue phlox at the center (various values and intensities secured from Sky Blue, Turquoise Blue and Light Blue over medium gray and light blue materials, and tints of Robin's Egg Blue over blue, dark gray and white) reflect the grayed blue background of draperies and the blues in two chairs. One of the phlox at the edge of the bouquet is in blue violets (two parts Aqua Pink and one part Violet over medium light blues for dark values; Light Blue and speck of Strawberry over gray, beige and white for medium values; Robin's Egg Blue over light blue for lightest values). The other one is in red violets (the same formulas of the blue violet over white, light beige and dark gray combined with natural red purple "as is" for dark values).

The tulips are a lovely plum, blending into soft gold edges (Plum over purple and ivory in varied intensities for dark values; two parts Aqua Pink and one part Violet over pale blue for light values; Gold over light gray, cream and white for edges).

Bachelor buttons are a combination of the red violets and blue violets. Poppies are red violet and the daisies and remaining flowers have the effect of being white, though their shadows vary from delicate chartreuse to bronze to golds.

The foliage is mostly blue-green (Reseda over greens; Reseda and Turquoise Green over gray for dark values; Green and Myrtle Green spot-dyed with Bronze over light blue and light gray for medium values; tints of Aqua Green and Myrtle Green over cream, white and light blue for highlights). There is quite a variation in the rose leaves, for some appear more yellow-green (Green over tans and light yellows, and Mint Green over light yellows and white). The phlox leaves blend from yellow-greens to gold edges.

FILIGREE

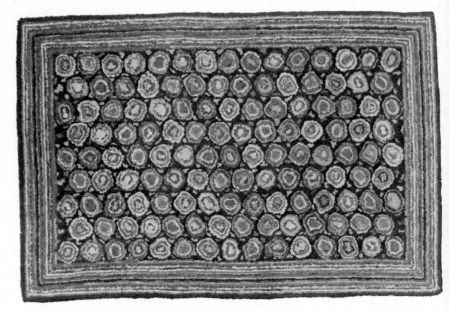

CAT'S PAW

"FILIGREE," hooked by Ada Maretti of Dorchester, Mass., Teacher, is an example of what a teacher does with a few simple suggestions by me, at one of our Teachers' Days. She had brought samples of her plain gray wallpaper, an aqua chair which was repeated in the painted bookshelves, and the reds of a sofa and rocker. The draperies in the room of her country home were off-white unbleached muslin.

The background is a very, very dark shade of red, a darker value than her sofa. The little leafy border to the octagons is veined and edged with varied aquas, and filled with paisley. Off-white formed the background within the vine lying next to the narrow border, which was edged with dark red and filled with paisley. Gray was used for the background around the fingered motif. The latter was edged with light aqua and filled with paisley, fingered back into darker reds. The little islands were edged with three values of the aqua and filled with paisley.

The intervening motif was edged with light aqua, and the body was blended from gray into off-white where it met the fingered center. The center was edged with dull red and filled with paisley. As a matter of fact, no dyeing was necessary for this rug, all the materials being colors which the average rugger usually collects.

"CAT'S PAW" was hooked by Elizabeth White of West Brookfield, Mass., under my supervision, in Sally Newhall's class. I had long wanted to work out the "Cat's Paw" in a medley of colors which would be gay but not garish. We started with a dark rich red background which was dyed irregularly so it fluctuated somewhat in its values, and was repeated for a space of three quarters of an inch at the edge of the rug.

In the development of the paws, a light value was used at the edge of each paw, so it would hold its own against the dark background. The light edge might be a delicate, soft rose pink, a sagey green, a soft aqua or even a very grayed lavender. The irregular areas of each paw were filled in a slightly different manner. For instance, with a grayed pink edge a grayed lavender was used next to it, then a gay green, a bright aqua, a dark, dull green, and a bit of brownish-gold, with a center of medium aqua. The next one would be outlined with a soft grayed green, and followed with a bright aqua, a grayed purple, soft rose pink, a bit of the gold and a sagey green center. Another might be edged with the pale grayed aqua, the deep aqua, the bright medium green, the brownish gold, the soft rose pink, and a filler in the center of a mixtured material. None of the colors were used in such a manner that they appeared spotty. Instead, each blended with jewel-like accents to form an interesting all-over effect. The little irregular marks between each paw were a chartreuse green, but even these varied slightly in value. The border was made up of single lines of all the varied colors used in the paws.

BASKET WEAVE

ALL RUGGERS accumulate a lot of odds and ends. The problem is, how may they be utilized and still achieve a rug of beauty? It can be done! "Basket Weave," hooked by Mrs. Floretta M. Brown of Dorchester, Mass., under my supervision, is one of two large geometrics used in the entrance hall of Rose Cottage. It was necessary to bind it to one already made, in which blue-greens dominated, and yet tie it up to an upholstery in a light grayed blue-green and mulberry. There was also a dull gold in the hall which had to be considered.

It was my desire to show, too, how attractive a geometric could be if a variety of mixtured materials were used with discrimination. I sorted all kinds of materials into two piles — in one those that might have any shade of green or blue-green and in the other anything that had the slightest cast of red-purple in it — regardless of whether they were light or dark, weak or bright, plain, plaid, tweeds or checks. There were many materials running into extremely light values of grays, tans, beige or almost white, or in which a thread or stripe of the color appeared.

The outer border and about three lines along the edges of all bands, lengthwise and crosswise, were hooked in black, and the little intervening blocks were an old creamy homespun blanket.

To repeat the gold in the hall, varied bright gold materials were used in the few dashing lines which were in the center of the bands in this pattern. When the other colors were hooked against these golds, their intensity was cut down, and yet the gold was subtly discernible.

The assortment of RPs were used in the lengthwise bands, but only one line of a material was used and carried completely along the band. Each line of hooking, thereafter, was of a different texture or material. Light was played against dark, and weak against bright, with an occasional gray, tan, beige or dirty white to give a fine "thready" effect.

In the crosswise bands, the BG assortment was used in the same manner, giving each band its own individuality.

Thus, a hodge-podge of materials may be bound together in a delightful and artistic manner if some thought is given to the combination of colors, and the manner in which they are applied.

Omár Kháyyám (small size)

THE LARGEST area in this smaller size of "Omár Kháyyám," hooked by Mrs. Clarence Sylvester of Brockton, Mass., Jeanne MacIver, Teacher, is the background under the large scroll surrounding the center medallion. Its lovely old blue has been carried over in several values to the flowers of the second border and those in the center of the medallion.

The second largest area is the corner background, which is of gold ivory. This is carried forward into the area between the two sets of scrolls surrounding the center medallion.

The third hue to be used in the greatest quantity is Maroon, which appears in the plain outside border. It is repeated in lighter values and weaker intensities in the background of the third border, in still lighter value and weak intensity for the inner background of the center medallion, and in the leafy scroll which cuts off the corners and surrounds the center medallion. Varied values of the maroon are blended into paisley, rose and Terra Cotta for the large scrolls that lie upon the old blue background, and for the floral detail in the corner. Notice how the textured paisley appears in various parts of these scrolls.

The circular center of the medallion repeats the paisley and all the hues in the rug, in varied values. The flowers surrounding it are of the old blues with leaves of varied yellow-greens.

The slender vine which separates the gold ivory background from the light center background is of the yellow-greens of the foliage, accented with gold.

Fringe has been added to impart an additional Oriental touch.

GAINSBOROUGH

In CERTAIN designs you may throw the spotlight of interest on either the scroll or the floral center. In "Gainsborough," hooked by Mrs. Sally W. Pollitt of Pascagoula, Miss., Alice J. Otis, Teacher, the plan was to emphasize the scroll and corners and play down the floral detail. Therefore, the roses and buds were of extremely moderate intensities and lighter values of equal parts of Crimson and Terra Cotta; chrysanthemums of equal parts of Gold and Old Gold; tulips and foxgloves a combination of two colors, Rose and Cherry for the pink shades, and Blue and Lavender for the purple shades. The foliage colors were secured from Myrtle, Reseda and Bronze Green, separate and combined, to give each type of leaf its own individuality. I think the fern leaves were quite delightful in the manner in which they were made. Each pinnate leaf is hooked with the underside green and the upperside of a soft grayed rose, and each one grows gradually lighter to end in a very light one.

Enough material was dyed for all the flowers and foliage, so that it would also make the scrolls. After the center was completed, all the left-over materials used in the floral center were over-dyed with Bronze, strong enough over each value to give it a definite bronze cast. The darker values were used for shadow accents, and the lighter values for tips and highlights. A great aunt's old blanket, creamy with age, was tint-dyed with Old Gold and Gold, and while still wet, spot-dyed with delicate tints of the colors in the floral bouquet, but not enough to change its general color from a very muted old gold. This was used as a filler for the parchment gold scroll.

The outside background was Mrs. Pollitt's son-in-law's old black dress suit and tuxedo. The inside background was her aunt's old white wool blanket. In fact, all the flower and foliage material was dyed over the same blanket.

Mrs. Pollitt said: "I have hooked seven rugs, and outside the cost of my patterns, I have spent only a dollar and a half for wool and that was only because I needed white. All materials I have used have been old blankets and garments collected from family and friends. Hooking rugs may be an expensive hobby if one buys all new wool, but from my experience it is about the most economical, worth-while hobby of which I know."

EARLY AMERICANA

THE FEELING of texture is given to "Early Americana," hooked by Mrs. Walter Comee of Canterbury, N. H., Geneva P. Foley, Teacher, by the small checks and plaids used in the border, scroll and varied detail of the center.

Onion skin dyeing played an important part in this rug. The background was a faded yellow blanket, over which she used Taupe, Mummy Brown and onion skins, all together in one dye bath, dyeing to secure three values. She used the lightest in the center, and gradually shaded out into the two slightly darker values in the remaining area.

Since this rug was made for a bedroom in an early American home, where the floors are of very wide boards, and the furniture is antique maple, an old-fashioned effect of mottling was given to the entire background and border. Small checks and plaids were dyed a darker value than that of the background, and used for the outside border and the center filler of the scroll. Old white flannel trousers broadly edged the scroll but was softened by a taupy off-white tweed where the edge of the scroll meets the background.

A tint of taupe with onion skins was used for a weak wash over all the floral and leaf dyeing. The Golds and Egyptian Reds of the large rose were carried forward into other flowers in a triangular balance. The dahlia and the small flowers at the ends were blended from Mummy Brown to creamy white. The berry-like flowers, which she calls pomegranates, and their balancing flowers, were made from Plum, Taupe and white, the pomegranates having rusty accents. The large center padula was of onion skin golds balanced by the large flower in profile and a morning glory.

The corner flowers differ, each repeating one of the important colors from the center. Some of the leaf detail was shaded from Gold to Bronze, down to grayed plum shadows, and other leaves were of Olive Green and Green over blues, with the addition of plum shadows.

The cornucopia was developed of the same materials as the scroll and the border.

What I like particularly about this rug is the way she has carried the white from her scrolls into the detail of the cornucopia and into the various parts of the floral detail, even into the corners.

SWEETHEART RUG

SPOT-DYED material is good to fill a small repeat scroll, like those in "Sweetheart Rug" hooked for me by Sally Newhall of Shirley, Mass., Teacher.

There is a delightful overtone to the entire color development because a little of the Strawberry dye, which was used for the carnations, has gone into everything else in the rug.

A very weak tint of it over taupe material forms the inner background, but only enough to give the taupe a warm cast. The center background, you will note, has been broken up by a delicate distinction of values that gives it a mosaic effect. A little more of the Strawberry dye went over the same taupe material to make it a little darker value at the edge. A still darker value fills the scrolls, which are outlined with a rather gay chartreuse green, spot-dyed so there is fluctuation in its values, thus avoiding a hard, sharp outline. The filler of the scroll is carried forward to the petals around the hearts. The heart is outlined with a tint of the carnation and filled with the inner background.

A little of the Strawberry was also spotted over light blue greens, and combined with stronger yellow-greens for the leafy detail, and for the four large scrolls at center sides. The brightest of yellow-green forms the centers of the carnations, which are made from several values of Strawberry with extremely light values at their edges, and a grayed Plum shadow at the base of each petal.

Notice my initials in one of the hearts? My grandson's (Jimmy) are in the other. The rug was made the year he was born, fourteen years ago, and when he is married my initials will be replaced with his bride's, and this will go into his home, I hope!

MATURITY

THE BLENDING of several dyes in one piece of material for floral detail made fascinating hooking in "Maturity" by Mrs. Charles E. Cleaves of Saco, Maine, Mary MacKay, Teacher.

Mrs. MacKay brushes her dyes together on a single strip of material. Since this is her own development, I will not trespass upon her methods. Perhaps sometime she will publish something along this line.

Here then is evidence of her artistry, where the Maroon shades of the roses are brushed into tints of Rust for the edges of the petals. Purples are brushed into medium values of Maroon, and then into delicate tints of rusty pinks for the tulips. The Rust and Maroon edges of the morning glories are brushed into a white and bronze throat. The tips of the white lilies are delicately tinted with Rust and Old Rose, and their petals have Bronze veins running into a bronze throat. Her dip-dyeing method of getting all the values necessary from dark shadows to very light highlights in one strip is applied to the dahlia.

Balance was carefully planned when I designed this pattern, so that if all the flowers are done in their one chosen hue wherever they appear, the repetition of color forms a good balance. Yet, in this interpretation, each flower has been given its own individuality by the use of a bit more shadow in one, and a little more highlight in another.

All the foliage is developed of closely blended gradation values in a variety of greens.

All of this lovely coloring is played against a rich background of purplish wine material, "as is."

If you analyze this color harmony, you will note that it travels from R through the warm hues almost around the Color Wheel to P, yet turns inward to subdued intensities of all the intervening hues.

TEACHERS' ANNUAL EXHIBIT, 1953

THIS "Fruit Scroll," hooked by Ruth McClellan of Shirley Center, Mass., Teacher, under supervision of Sally Newhall, Teacher, was an experiment in hooking a rug that would have the stenciled appearance as that of her cabinet and chairs. All our regular rules and principles had to be laid aside to follow, instead, the rules of stenciling.

To give the background the effect of reddish streaks showing through painted wood, she used Terra Cotta over Oxford gray, Navy over scarlet (for highlights), and most important, red and black buffalo check, dyed with Dark Green for darkest shades. These were hooked in slightly curved horizontal strokes, to give the "grained" effect. All the details had interrupting lines of background, stencil fashion. The fruit colors were like stencil powders, gold, aluminum, copper, purple and bright green, which produced a grayed rosy peach, grayed plums and grapes, and pears of brassy green.

The dull gold scroll was played down into the background. It must appear sharp and clean cut on all edges, and be shadowed in the center of its larger areas, as if the background was showing through. The idea was to have the gold look dirty and dull, and Mrs. McClellan said: "I certainly came up with a drab looking bunch of rags."

In the "Daphne" (to the right), hooked by Mrs. Robert Maher of Springfield, Mass., Emma Urban, Teacher, who would believe that Kelley green material crowded into a Garnet dye bath would develop a very lovely dark brownish-red outer background, while Fireman's red material crowded into a Dark Green dye bath provided a slightly lighter and richer brownish-red inner background?

Taupe is an overtone in the floral detail. The dominant rose is one part Taupe, two parts Terra Cotta, and four parts Coral over beige and white. Taupy white daisies slide subtly into Violet shadowy accents, with center of brownish-yellow slightly tinged with Cardinal and Taupe. Morning glories of soft Turquoise Blue are tinged with Bronze. The foliage of yellow-green has an overtone of Mummy Brown. Mummy Brown and Bronze form the border lines, outlined with Old Gold.

The "Daphne" (to the left), hooked by Mrs. Paul L. Willson of Saco, Maine, Mary MacKay, Teacher, was developed in an analogous harmony of YRs, swinging slightly toward R and YG with just a bit of complementary B. The background is dark brown. The rose is Terra Cotta, blending into yellows and tints of Bronze, for its highlights. The tints of Bronze are also carried over into the daisies which are of Green over delicate yellow and white, with gold centers shadowed with dull purple. A cool note appears in the morning glories, which blend from deep blue at the edges, blending quickly into very light values of bluish-white and tints of Bronze. The rose leaves and sepals of the rosebuds are shadowed with dull purple. The band repeats four to five values of the bronzy-yellows.

PLUME

FLORAL detail does not always have to be in high color. In fact, there are times when it is quite necessary to use extremely low intensity bordering on the neutral, relying on intensities in extremely small areas. This is the plan of "Plume," hooked by Ruth Higgins of Ellsworth, Maine, Teacher, where the rug is one of several made in similar colorings, to be used together in one room.

The color plan is a complementary of R and BG, with the addition of one of the near complements of YR. All the dyeing was over white and light beiges, as follows:

R ⎰ Cardinal with bit of Mahogany.
⎱ Mahogany with a bit of Silver Gray and a very light tint of Cardinal.

YR Mahogany and very little Orange (keeping it brown if possible).

BG Green, Peacock and very little Jade.

Ten to fourteen shades of each color were dyed to get a good range to choose from. In this way Mrs. Higgins developed dark, medium and even white flowers from just one color.

After the dyeing was done, an overtone was given to all the greens by dipping them for a short time in varied strengths of Mahogany dye, the lightest values in delicate tints, and the darker values in gradually stronger solutions, but only enough to soften them.

The background was a soft gray diagonal weave, crowded into a delicate bath of Mahogany, using slightly darker values from slightly stronger dye for the area under the floral detail in the center, and for the outer background.

In applying this color, the roses were from the Rs and YRs; some flowers were YRs with the Rs in the shadows; no flower is of one hue only; every flower and the leaves, too, have some R in them, either as shadow or highlight, in what she terms "Titivating." "In other words," she says, "after a flower is hooked, I pick up the edges of petals with a white or very light pink."

The scrolls of almost neutral YRs have an almost white edge with a pinky tinge and are darkest near their BG veins.

Imagination is shown in the blue-green leaves which turn to Mahogany-pinks on one side. Some are veined in self colors, while others are in the complementary Rs.

Mrs. Higgins says: "I got as much vanity into the leaves as I could."

WATER NYMPH

THE RUGMAKER'S SONG

MAKING a rug fit into its surroundings is an interesting project, but when it is also to be used in the home of a beloved daughter, it takes on additional meaning.

"Water Nymph," hooked by Mrs. Harry Coley of West Boylston, Mass., Eva Bonci, Teacher, repeats in its background an important color in the room, a very pale watery blue from boiling blue material of strong intensity in a detergent.

The lilies were developed from a wide variety of values and intensities — some blending from Pink to Lavender to Plum, some from dark Strawberry to delicate tints of Cardinal, and some of delicate Maize shading into shadows of Mahogany.

The lily pads were grayed greens, shading from light into darker values at edge. The treatment of the seaweed was interesting, in that it was not too dominant. Its stem, which also forms the under part of each curling extremity, was deep Mahogany. The outer irregular edge of each curl was soft grayed yellow, and the remaining space between was filled in with a yellow and reddish-brown fine check.

THE BLACK background of "The Rugmaker's Song," hooked by Mrs. Arthur Kohn of Toledo, Ohio, Bernice Decker, Teacher, dramatizes the coral red poppies and taupy white snow drops, with soft yellow-green foliage. The scrolls are of grayed Terra Cottas, with a bit of Mummy Brown added. The design was inspired by my neighbor's poem:

THE RUG MAKER

"I envy an artist," the woman said,
As into the pattern she hooked her thread,
"I envy a poet," the woman thought,
As into a rug the pattern was wrought.
"An artist can paint such wonderful things
And a poet can tell his dreams as he sings."
And as she belittled, her fingers worked on,
She did not know she was making a song!

The wools at her feet in sweet disarray
Were like threads of her life, some drab, some gay.
She thought of her youth and the love of her heart,
Whilst she wove a poppy, blood-red from the start.
She thought of the heartaches she'd known on the way,
And a border of snow drops crept in to stay.
Each leaf must be perfect, each tendril complete,
Like a baby's fingers, so precious and sweet.

"I envy a poet," still she said,
And the rug was finished, a poem in thread.
"I envy an artist," she continued to scoff,
While the rug lay in glory, a "Rembrandt" in cloth!

— *Jane Goyer*

GLORIA

"GLORIA," hooked by Mrs. F. B. Sundstrom of Worcester, Mass., Eleanor Loftus, Teacher, was made for a new home. Therefore, the colors of her room and its furnishings will be planned around the rug.

The background is of taupe, and since taupe belongs to the red family, and the scrolls are also of red, it was necessary to use a tint of Green dye over it, to gray it down somewhat, and be a good contrast for the scrolls.

The red scroll was made up of many odds and ends left from other rugs, some of it being re-dyed Maroon, some of it in Terra Cottas, depending upon the material over which it was dyed. Some of it came from bright reds that had been bled, and gray materials were put into the same pot so they took on tinges of the red and provided weak intensities. If it was too bright, it was dulled with Green dye. The plan was to keep it muted and soft, so it would sink away somewhat and become unimportant in the background.

Since the red background and scroll ruled out colorful roses, a gradation of shades were made of extremely grayed Greens in a vertical path up to pure white for these roses. The tulips blended from dull reds into very weak golds. The large padulas of a grayed pinkish-white with grayed accents at base of petals were thus kept in close relationship to the main hue.

The duller and slightly darker reds, used for the small clusters of flowers between the scrolls and in the center, were repeated in the ribbon. The tiny buds in the outer area of the bouquet, being a small area, are gold and are reflected in the tips of many of the leaves between the scrolls and in the center bouquet.

Notice the delightful contrast of dark and light values in the scrolls, the ribbon and the floral center.

MEMORIA

THE KEY to the whole coloring of this "Memoria," hooked by Mrs. Elizabeth Shroyer, Kansas City, Kansas, Mrs. Margaret Hunt, Teacher, is in the grayed raisin background (two parts Ecru and one part Taupe over medium gray).

The roses blend from creamy tints of Ecru in their highlights into dusty rose and deep Mahogany shadows. The tulips repeat the Mahoganies and dusty pinks at their edges, shading quickly back into extremely light tints of the Ecru at their base.

The jonquils are hooked in subdued Golds and Khaki, shadowed with Taupe at the base of the cup. Lighter values at the edges make them "flute."

The lily nearest the center is a very grayed Gold with Taupe shadows at center and where the fore petal curls back, while the one near the outer area of the bouquet takes on the Ecru cast of the rose.

The iris is a grayed PB in the upper petals and a dark, richer PB in its falls.

The other flowers, except the gray-white pussy willows, are blended from light tints into either the dusty rose or Mahogany (Taupe dye with Mahogany added), or into varied PB shades (Taupe with Blue dye added) and the latter are somewhat intensified, especially in the pansies and violets.

All the foliage is played down in rather dark YGs (Gold, Khaki and Bronze Green), or of BGs, the latter softened with Khaki, both darkened and dulled, when necessary, with Taupe.

The inner side of the scroll repeats the dull BGs of the foliage, shading into lighter values at the leafy tips, with dusty rose and Mahogany knobs. The outer side repeats the YGs of the foliage, blending into extremely light values of Ecru and Khaki. Thus you will notice how often the Khaki and Ecru have been used to give an overtone to the entire rug, which gives unity to the color plan as a whole.

LUCETTA'S TREE OF LIFE

IMAGINATION is quite necessary in developing any design like "Lucetta's Tree of Life," hooked by Mrs. Bernard D. Colton of Portland, Maine, Erline Stearns, Teacher, because so much of the detail is fanciful.

Mrs. Colton has succeeded in binding all of its fantasy together by having a wide range of values and intensities from her dyeing, and by combining all of her varied hues in many different ways in its fanciful floral detail. Dyeing is her hobby, so she has a record of her experience, and when you see how many values and intensities she uses, you will understand why her rug is so beautiful. This is what she has used:

Mahogany:	3 values over white, 1 dark, 1 medium and 1 light.
Egyptian Red:	8 values over gray and 12 values over white.
Terra Cotta:	5 values over gray and 12 values over white.
Brown Rust:	6 values over white.
Brown:	7 values over pale yellow and 9 values over white.
Bronze:	4 values over white.
Olive Green:	5 values over pale yellow and 6 values over white.
Khaki:	9 values over white.
Aqua:	7 values over gray and white.
Plum:	11 values over gray, pink and white.
Myrtle Green:	6 values over white.
Bright Green	
Olive Green	mixed: 5 values over white.
Hunter's Green	
Chartreuse:	5 values over white.

Nugget Gold with bit of Purple: 9 values over white.
Silver Gray with bit of Egyptian Red: 5 values over white.

All the coloring in the border, basket and lower corners comes from shades in the first seven dyes. Darkest of Mahogany formed the outside border and inside background.

Many from the group of seven were repeated in various ways, and used with the last eight in the center. It is repetition over and over again, carrying forward the general hue of one detail into some small accent or highlight of another that gives unity to this whole color plan.

When analyzed, this appears to be a varied color harmony, including practically all the hues except RP and B, but you will notice from the colored illustration that all the intensities are extremely moderate, unless they are used in a very small area.

Amish

Strawberry Patch

The Dye Dabbler provides definite color plans for certain designs like "Amish." However, it may be changed to suit your own fancy, as in this one hooked by Mrs. Richard Wilde of Northford, Conn., Rose Pimm, Teacher. In this Pennsylvania Dutch design of bright colors and no subtle shadings, one has to follow different principles in developing its detail.

Mrs. Wilde uses reds from Maroon and Scarlet; varied blues from Navy, Royal, Peacock and Blue, aside from blue tweed mixtures, and for the third hue, Golds dyed over plain and mixtured materials. They are used over and over again — sometimes for filler and sometimes for outline — contrasting one color against another in its varied detail. Navy Blue and Peacock edge the light grayed-blue tweed background of the wide border. The inner background is off-white, an old blanket. The leaves rising from the scarlet heart are varied, from dark green at the base to gold tweed, maroon, scarlet and yellow for the light top ones. The tulips are in the blues so often seen in Amish colorings; the pineapples in the golden yellows with maroon accents, and the large flat flowers on the vines at both ends of the grayed-blues. The urns are blue with gold accents at the top. The carnations in the border are of scarlet and dark gray, and the foxgloves of gold tweeds, yellows and grays. The petals of the hex signs are scarlet, and the scalloped edges are maroon, filled with green.

This "Strawberry Patch," hooked by Mrs. Dorothy Gailey of Providence, R. I., Teacher, under my supervision in Sally Newhall's class, is developed in accordance with the color suggestions of Dye Dabbler #40. The background is antique black, except for the little diamonds under the strawberry blossoms, which are an extremely dark yellow-green, repeated in the outer border. The white blossoms are shadowed with grays and have soft brownish-yellow centers. The berries vary, some being of the rich, luscious reds (Cardinals over beige and white, plus Turkey red material "as is"); others turning to yellowish tips with an occasional one turning to a greenish-white tip. A soft gold forms the seeds of the berries.

The leaves are blue-green with dark red veins and have occasional tips or jagged edges of red (not as a continuous line, but a few little loops here and there, providing repetition from the red berries). Those which curl over have a light underside to the leaf, with an extremely light highlight at the edge which lies next to the deeply shadowed upper part of the leaf. The stems are yellow-greens.

The hexagon border of the larger spray is in three dark values of blue-greens (Green over grays and whites), and the hexagon border of the smaller spray in three lighter values of the same blue-greens.

THOUGHTS OF LOVE

SCROLLS may be extremely interesting if you use plenty of dark shadow, contrasted with highlight in their development. "Thoughts of Love," hooked by Ethel Bull of Auburn, Mass., Teacher, is an excellent example of this, and shows how a good color plan is improved by imagination. While she has a simple, almost monochromatic effect (except for. her contrasting foliage), she has extended into neighboring hues for emphasis and exaggeration in very small details, to give her plan unusual character.

The background, which covers the greater area of this design, is a warm taupe, "as is," that bound itself beautifully with the Mahogany dye which was used in most of the detail.

Mahogany dye in various strengths was used over grays, pinks and very light beiges and white for both scrolls and flowers. Every flower has an overtone of mahogany or pink, even the pussy willows. More of the dark values were used in developing the iris. The medium light values were emphasized for the daffodils, which have delicate edges and accents of gold. The lightest values were used for the dogwood, with gold centers, and the pussy willows. But notice how she has enriched the dark values in the iris, and added a bit of intensity of soft golds and yellows in the daffodils. A tinge of pink in the white dogwood and pussy willows gives additional relationship.

Notice, too, Mrs. Bull's delightful contrast in the development of the scrolls, from extremely dark values at their knobby ends, subtly blending into medium values for the general body of the scroll, turning to almost white at their tips with delicate tints of Mahogany and green for accents. Their veins have been made very unimportant by repeating varied values of taupy-browns of the background.

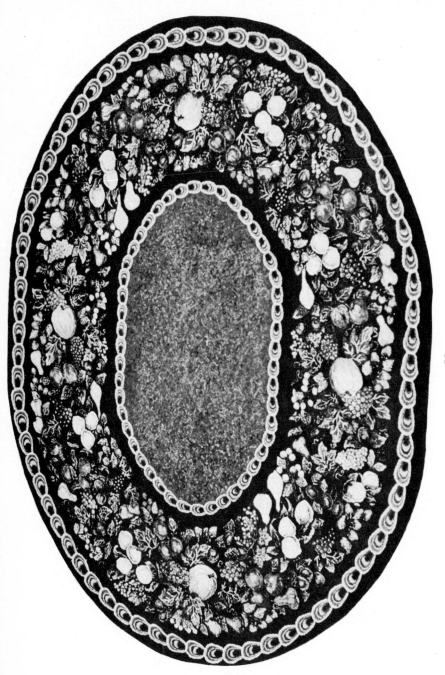

DISCRIMINATION was used in playing down much of the fruit in "Harvest" hooked by Hazel Snow of Bakersfield, Calif., Viola Shultz, Teacher. The general effect of this rug is a rich and dark reddish brown background (Mahogany dye to which smaller amounts of Red Grape, Wood Rose and Plum were added and dyed over medium to dark grays), with somewhat subdued coloring in most of the detail. However, a glow of gold crops out in the peacock borders, melons, grapes, peaches, pears and gourds. In fact, a bit of gold or goldish-green has been carried into the dye of almost every leaf or fruit in this development. Every color has something of another color added to it, either in the dyepot or in the blending of the colors. Mrs. Shultz likes to dye all kinds of detail in the same dyepot to give it relationship. The center background is of slightly lighter values than that under the fruit. A little Black has been added to the background dye of the area beyond the outside peacock border.

The peacock scroll border is made up of seventeen shades, and blends from a center of deep reddish-purple into lighter values. Then it is contrasted with soft greens and edged with greenish-gold.

The golds are reflected in various values and intensities in the melons, peaches, pears (with blushing cheeks) and gourds, and a few greenish-yellow grapes. The very dark rich red apples sink somewhat away into the dark background. Their highlights appear in very small spaces near the center of the apples. Brighter intensities of their reds are repeated in the strawberries and currants, and the lighter values but grayer intensities are in the cherries. The grapes are in three different hues — some in the plum-purples, some in the grayed reddish-purples, and others in grayed-blues. The plums are extremely grayed plum shades. The leaf detail has considerable individuality, being in both blue-greens and yellow-greens. This was Mrs. Snow's fourth rug. It may be interesting to the reader to know it was entirely made on a small box frame and moved about on it as her work progressed. It was completed within a year.

Sea Grapes

THE DESIGN for "Sea Grapes," hooked by Ruth Jones of the Hookrafter's Guild, under my supervision, was inspired by the sea grape shrub which is so prevalent in Southern Florida, and contains its foliage, fruit and flower.

The predominance of BGs gives it something of a monotone effect, although small amounts of a near complement (RP) and a distant hue (soft goldish-yellow very near the neutral pole) give additional interest and "oomph" to the color plan as a whole.

I desired to show only a subtle difference in the background of the alternate blocks. The lighter ones are tints of Old Gold and Silver Gray over almost whitish material, while the darker ones are about equal tints of Silver Gray and Khaki Drab over the same material.

The leaves are many values of moderate intensity of enough Old Gold over various blue materials to give them blue-green shades and tints. They shade darkest at their base or where an edge has curled over. The curled edges are in the near complement of RP. The grapes are generally of the same color as the leaves, except that brighter intensities have been used because of their small areas. You will note that to keep the modern effect each grape is hooked in just one value. It is flat, with no shadow or highlight. One loop of the RP has been pulled into most of the grapes to indicate the blossom ends, and serves as an additional subtle repetition of the stem and vein colors.

The exaggerated stem changes from dark values of Maroon into Red Grape, and thence into a softer and lighter Rose, where they form the division line between the irregular blocks that lead to their blossoms. When they enter into and become the veins of the leaves, they spread at their extremities into soft golds and yellows.

Their little blossoms, which are of a very small area, are hooked one at a time with a few loops of pure white, and then one loop of gold and one loop of purple (for shadows) are hooked into the center. In this way it does not grow confusing.

The darker values of the leaves are used for the border.

HOME IN THE WILDERNESS

(*An adaptation of Currier & Ives*)

PERSPECTIVE is one of the most important points to keep in mind when hooking a pictorial, because you are really painting a picture. Therefore, all the colors in the distance must be grayed and muted to give the effect of remoteness. Those in the foreground can be of the brighter intensities.

In this "Home in the Wilderness," hooked by Mrs. Hallie Hall of Great Neck, N. Y., Teacher, this important point and many other details have been carefully planned in advance.

As all artists know, you must first establish from which direction the light hits the picture, and this question having been settled, the principle must be followed consistently. Thus, in this one, the imaginary sun comes in from the left, behind the large tree. This brought the full emphasis on the cabin and its immediate surroundings. The mother, the little girl and the chickens are in gay colors, and a golden highlight strikes part of the open barrel. The figures further from the cabin are a bit more quiet. If bright intensities are used, such as in the mittens or a cap, it is in a much smaller area than those in the foreground. The cabin is all sorts of golden browns and light beiges, with its crevices in darkest browns, with even an accent of black, particularly under the eaves. Black is used in the open doorway.

The effect of the forest was secured through extremely grayed shades from the dyepot, through "layer dyeing" of many of the colors used in the rest of the picture, such as Old Gold, Silver Gray, Olive Green and Seal Brown — putting the darkest pieces at the bottom and the lightest at the top. As the colors steamed through, the lower pieces took on the dark, dusky shades necessary behind the log cabin, and the tints worked in beautifully in the clouds.

All the colors in the distance are grayed and softened.

On the right, the distant sky, looking through the trees, seems grayish-green, but toward the left side whitish clouds appear at the tops of the trees, against a sky of delicate lavender-blue.

The evergreens seem a little nearer to the eye because they are of definite blue-greens against the grayed horizon.

The dark gray trunks of trees in the foreground have textured materials that give them a "barky" effect. An interesting note is the mingling of varied shades of grays, gray-blues and browns which are streaked into the lower right corner of the picture, along its base, and in the lower left before it rises to the higher elevation. This makes a smooth transition into the dark border which is black — a single line of gold within.

Everyone will see this picture differently. The joy of color is that you can apply it in the way in which it will bring *you* the greatest satisfaction!

FLETCHER GEOMETRIC

A COMPLEMENTARY contrast of mahoganies and blue-greens has been used in "Fletcher Geometric" hooked by Edna Fleming of North Easton, Mass., Teacher. She has also used the diagonal path from dark rich to light dull shades and tints in both hues.

Only two dyes were used, a variation of Mahoganies and a variation of Reseda Greens. The very darkest value of her Mahogany has been used for the outside border, the background under the main motif, and at the center of all the petals. A slightly lighter value has been used for the background area between the main motifs and the border, and a still lighter value has been used for background under the intervening motif. Although the values are close, there is enough difference to intrigue the eye.

The lighter values of Mahogany have been used as the petals in all the main motifs, shading from a dark rich up to a light weak mixture. The edges of these petals have been outlined with a light grayed aqua that had a little mahogany thread. This has been repeated at the inside edge of the border of the main motif, and for little broken lines of color within the border.

The Reseda Greens have been used for the border of the main motif, darker values along the inner side, slightly lighter values in the outer part. Buried among the darker values is an occasional broken line of the darkest value of the Mahogany.

In the intervening motif the petals have been developed from dark values of the blue-greens to light grayed tints at their edges. These have been outlined with a gray, mahogany and white tiny plaid, which has been repeated at the outer edge of the main motif. The definite difference between the light grayed aqua mixture with a mahogany thread, and the gray, mahogany and white tiny plaid is almost dissipated when hooked. Yet each is related to the two hues used so that the aqua one against the mahogany petals and the mahogany one against the Reseda petals is an extremely subtle touch.

There is a little variation in the conventional petals which makes them that much more interesting.

It is an extremely simple application of two complementaries, and yet shows how delightful simplicity can be when two hues are applied in pleasing intensities and values to a design.

LAGARZA

"Lagarza," hooked by Mrs. Sarah R. Hubbard of Detroit, Mich., Bernice K. Decker, Teacher, is a replica of the boat which first discovered Bermuda.

Motion has been given to its development by the directional lines of hooking in the swirling lines and dark accents of the sails which indicate they are full of wind, and in the water, which swoops and throws its whitecaps against the boat.

All the materials used for this pictorial were gray, tans, taupes or browns. The colors were removed from some of them, and strong dyes were used over the other dull shades to get the desired colors. Mahogany and Seal Brown, accented with black, were used for the bands on the side of the boat, and Mummy Brown over tan for the wood of the boat, to resemble oak, the latter being used again for the ropes. Various values of Mummy Brown, tans, creamy white and deep taupe made the sails bulge. Two-thirds Mummy Brown and one-third Terra Cotta were used over the tans and taupes for the outside of the shield, the lions (on the sails), the cabin roof and part of the fore flag. Varied grays with black accents fashioned the doors and windows, the anchor and the cannon.

For the ocean, a sequence of values of Ocean Green, Turquoise Green and Blue were dyed, and a plaid containing navy, aqua and black was used in very small quantities for emphasis. A plaid skirt of blue, yellow and gray was used for the lower part of the sky, the blue and yellow at the horizon blending into the blue alone, and thence to the gray of the clouds, which were heavily tipped with white. Above the clouds the sky was grayed-blue. The aft flag was of light values of Maroon and dark Mummy Brown from the sails. A greenish-blue top flag had a Terra Cotta cross and shadow accents of dark blue. Dark blue, steel gray and black made the pirate flag. The shield within the Mummy Brown and Terra Cotta frame had a whitish background, and the lettering was in the blues of the ocean.

The border was greenish-blue (like the top flag) at the edge, with a line of white separating it from a few lines of Terra Cotta and one line of black at the inner edge.

GODDESS OF FORTUNA

A DOUBLE complementary harmony of RP–R and G–BG with P and GY was used for "Goddess of Fortuna" hooked by Lillian Knight and Ruth Jones (members of Hookrafter's Guild), under my supervision, for a beautiful home on Lake Michigan.

The outside background of antique blackish-green is dark green material dulled down with Maroon dye. The inside background of warm cream is Champagne dye with a bit of Mahogany over white.

The dominating scrolls cover a very large area. A great number of values were dyed for a good gradation of moderate and weak intensities from the darkest values in the twist of the knobs and along the mid-ribs to the lightest at the tips. The darkest values of the GY scroll (which crosses the G–BG scroll) are from Bronze Green, Khaki Drab and Olive Green dyes over medium to light grays. The lightest are tints of Nile and Bronze (separate and together) over white.

The dyes used for the G–BG scroll are Reseda, Turquoise Green and Green, and are used over grays, blues and mixtures. Their gradation follows a diagonal path from dark bright to light dull. They take on an additional interest in their tips, which flow into tints of the complementary flower colors from the corners. Thus, some of the tips of the GY scroll, which is veined with Purple, turn to tints of Purple, at their extremities, repeating the hue of the tulip.

The G–BG scroll (veined with Maroon) flows into light grayed aqua and thence into accented edges of tints of Maroon in some of their extremities, repeating the color of the rose.

Tints of Maroon and Purple are combined for the petunias, and darker and duller intensities of them are used for the long ferny detail in opposite corners.

The cornucopia is developed of slightly brighter intensities of the G–BGs.

Notice how the colorful tips of the scroll balance each other. Notice, too, that your decision as to where a darker outer background is to change to a dramatic lighter one, will affect the design. In this particular pattern, if dramatic changes are to be made in the two backgrounds, unless you carry the lighter one in under the scroll detail at both ends, as in this illustration, you would lose some of the feathery effect of the scrolls and your center background would tend toward becoming a squarish rectangle.

CALLA LILY WREATH

I HAVE always considered it not only a pleasure, but an obligation to purchase finished rugs which would be a help and inspiration to you. Thus, when an unusually fine rug comes into the market, my purchase of it is my way of saying, "Thank you for your patronage. Now come and enjoy some of the fruits of it."

"Calla Lily Wreath" is one of these rugs. It was hooked by Gertrude Longley of Plainfield, Mass. While she had had no lessons on this particular rug, she pays tribute to her teacher, Helen Hill of Williamsburg, Mass., who had taught her to make one similar to it. Mrs. Longley says: "I do think she should have the credit." It is refreshing to hear a woman say this, for many times pupils fail to give teachers due credit.

Its colors are very similar to the color plan of the Dye Dabbler. The background was a soft blue material put through a dye bath of weak Myrtle Green and a little Silver Gray that gave it a medium value of very grayed blue-green. The inner background was a tint of Silver Gray over dirty white.

The grapes were Red Grape and Rose over various materials, including purples, blues and orchids. The resulting colors that leaned toward purple were used in the corner clusters, with an occasional grape of rose. Those that tended toward rose were used at the two ends and center sides, with an occasional one of green. The remaining clusters were of varied greens, with an occasional one of light grayed lavender. A very subtle repetition! Notice how several of the yellow-green leaves are blended from deeper shades at center veining to light edges, while the other side blends from light values to darker edges. The corner leaves are a much grayer green of light value and have a dull brownish edge. The tendrils are light against the outer dark background, and those lying against the inner background change from green to grayed reds as they twist or curl.

The floral wreath is a varied color harmony, with RP dominating. The fuchsias, pansies and small padulas are in the deep RPs and the little cluster of three padulas is a PB. The roses have white petals heavily shadowed with mulberry pink, and the calla lilies have taupy gray shadows around the gold pistils. Gold and chartreuse gleam jewel-like in flower center, stamens and tips of leaves.

When I first saw the rug, the calla lilies were so near the value of the background that one could hardly detect them. At my suggestion, Mrs. Longley shadowed the background with taupy shades, which, as you will see, bring out the lovely contrasting white petals.

[267]

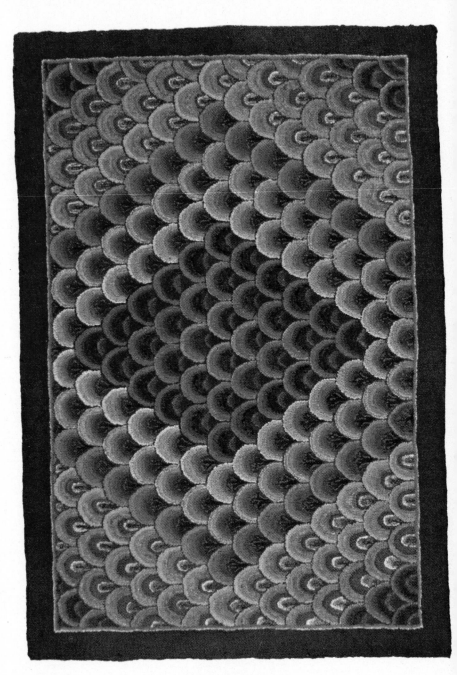

VERMONT SHELL

"VERMONT SHELL," hooked by Grace O'Neil of Fitchburg, Mass., Teacher, is a harmony of near complements of:

(1) R (Maroon dye over light beige materials in about five values);

(2) G (Olive Green dye over same light beige materials in about five values);

(3) Varied beige and taupe materials "as is," without dyeing, for the three lightest values, and the same materials dyed in weak Maroon to give them just a little cast of color for two dark values serve to bring the two near complements together in harmony.

A geometric of small repeating figures may take on glamour and interest through slight differences in the application of values used in this manner: the two darkest shades of #3 were used for the center base of the six center shells (running both ways) and blended into the gradation of reds. In the four center shells, more of the two lighter values were used at the outer curve.

In the next three rows surrounding the red shells, three little stems were hooked at the base of green, with two or three loops of light maroon on their tops. Then the darker values of #3 were hooked in remaining base of these shells, blended into the lighter taupes and beige. Among them was a gray mixture with a mahogany thread in it that gave additional interest. More of the light values were used in the row next to the red shells, each row growing subtly darker as it extended outward.

In the following three rows a little thumb print of the lightest tint of Maroon (over a plaid) was used at the base of each shell; then blended from dark green base to a very light, soft green edge. Again the row next to the taupes had more of the light values, growing gradually darker in each row outward.

The remaining corner shells repeated the red development of the center.

Three lines of varied taupes outlined the inner edge of the border, the latter being of the darkest Maroon.

Thus the dark taupes were repeated in the red shells — tiny accents of red and green were repeated in the taupe shells — and tints of the red were repeated in the green shells, pulling all three together.

SYMMETRY

This "Symmetry," hooked by Mrs. Mae Bacon of Leicester, Mass., under my supervision, was made as a companion for a "Duke of Marlborough" and a "Gainsborough."

The background of an extremely dark brown repeated those in the other two rugs.

The scrolls were "painted," some shading from the soft blue-green, which dominated in this color plan, to a very grayed cinnamon brown, out to taupy white or slightly Apricot tips. Others shaded from a very dark taupy gray to a dull green, then blue, and finally a bluish-white tip. Some turned from a dark slaty taupe into browns, then into greens, blues, into small curling knobs of the tints of the color with which they began. Others blended from soft grayed greens into tawny tans, and thence into soft yellowish-cream. The smallest ones went from taupe into delicate bluish-white tips; or from browns into taupes and thence into dirty white tips. They were all veined with varied RPs, which gave repetition to the color plan.

The general colors of one scroll were repeated in other scrolls, in such a way as to give something of a triangular balance.

The secret in "painting" a scroll is blending from one color into another by using the same value and intensity of the two colors where they meet. The transition may be made in any of the values. Thus, a dark knob of brown can turn to a dark yellow-green before the scroll begins to lighten. Or a medium value of green in the middle area of a scroll may be fingered into a medium value of blue, but of the same intensity.

In this plan, however, the scrolls changed in value generally from a dark knob to medium values near the middle area of a scroll, to lighter tips or knobs.

An additional note of interest was given to those scrolls which had several smaller knobs at their extremities, by balancing the knobs in a triangular manner, and using the colors of a near-by scroll.

Colors blend easiest when their sequence of color follows their order around the Color Wheel.

PERFUME BOX

"PERFUME BOX," hooked by Vida Jopson of West Hartford, Conn., Teacher, is a good example of a split complementary harmony.

Its detail is played against a creamy white background (an old blanket unchanged by dye). The carnations are the brightest intensity, being a deep, rich red (Cardinal dyed over pink material). The hibiscus are a lighter value and are a little less intense (of Cherry), with dark thumb print, like the carnation, at the base of the petals. Their long pistils are a much lighter value (shadowed on both sides by the dark red) with tiny caps to their fuzzy gold stamens of deep, rich red. The phlox is a mixture of the reds from both carnations and hibiscus, in varied values and intensities, with extremely dark red accents at the base of each petal. Thus, all the flowers in this pattern are developed of one hue.

The carnation leaves are aqua, just as it came from the mill, but to give them more interest, two values of blue were spot-dyed with weak Bronze dye for shadows and veining.

The hibiscus leaves are yellow-green, from strong Reseda (with a little Yellow and Buttercup Yellow added), over a gray-green material for the dark value; medium Aqua Green over beiges, with a little Buttercup added for medium values and Old Gold over beige and white for lightest values. The small phlox leaves are Old Gold over beige, veined with aqua.

The yellow-greens of the hibiscus leaves are used for the outer and inner bands of the corners which also form diamonds in the border. Their values are hooked in such a manner as to form broken lines of intensity.

The aqua blues used in the carnation leaves form the two center bands of the corners, and also form diamonds in the same manner. Notice how Mrs. Jopson always adds her initials and the year in which she makes her rug.

SCROLL FROM "SYMMETRY"

SOUTHERN BELLE

TEACHERS are so busy they seldom have the time to make or finish rugs of their own. Yet they feel the need to keep in constant touch with new ideas, which may be worked out on smaller pieces.

This scroll from "Symmetry" was hooked by Mrs. Walter A. Towe of Ridgewood, N. J., Teacher, as an experiment in blending from dark, rich maroons into lighter rose and delicate pinks, and making a transition into delicate blues (tints of Copenhagen Blue) and blue-lavenders (tints of Violet) in knobby ends. Its very light background was spotted with delicate tints of all the dyes used in the rug. She very cleverly changed the rectangle outline of the pattern to a swirling border line, irregularly darkened with the dark values of the scroll, which gave it a modern effect.

A MODERN monotone effect was given "Southern Belle," hooked by Ann Jorgensen of Fresno, Calif., Lillian Ayres, Teacher, by low intensities of Wood Rose and Seal Brown dyes. The magnolias of a pinkish beige were blended from gradation dyeing of Wood Rose to which only a little Seal Brown was added over white and beige. Notice how beautifully the petals curl over by the subtle shading of various values used for shadows. The foliage of a warm brown was a gradation of Seal Brown, to which a little Wood Rose was added.

Darker warm brown materials "as is" were used for the outer border and a slightly lighter value for the background of the outer area around the floral detail. The larger inner area of background, which has a fluctuation of values, was an outworn bathrobe of a similar rosy brown, which had a broad, very subtle stripe. It was cut crosswise, so that, as it was hooked, the slightly lighter values constantly rose to the surface and gave it this fluctuation. How clever of her to use it only in this larger area where it would not detract the eye from the detail!

EARTH'S ENDOWMENT

"EARTH'S ENDOWMENT," hooked by Muriel Borden of Haverhill, Mass., Sally Newhall, Teacher, was planned for a wall hanging in the dining room of the new home of her daughter. When I first met Mr. Borden, he said proudly: "It is the most beautiful rug I have ever seen." Its border was Olive Green with a little Myrtle Green over beige. The inner background was a homespun blanket "as is." The little branches that form frames for the fruit were Taupe blended into Silver Gray, with a streak here and there of Reseda Green.

The fruit was an all-color harmony of the following:

1. The purple grapes and plums were from Plum and Aqualon Pink.
2. The peach, pear and apricots were of Apricot, Mummy Brown and Aqualon Yellow, with tinges of Cardinal and Egyptian Red for blushes, and these same dyes were used for the strawberries.
3. Crab apples, cherries and raspberries were of Burgundy and Garnet, with tints of it over pale yellow providing highlights.
4. The melon was of Green with a little Copenhagen Blue for the shadows, blended into gradations of Reseda, Olive Green and a little Myrtle, down to a grayed Chartreuse.
5. The blueberries were from Blue blended into tints of Copenhagen and Aqualon Blue, and Navy was used for the background under the berries.
6. The pineapple was a blend of Seal Brown, Medium Brown, Mummy Brown, Aqualon Yellow and Chartreuse, with "eyes" of Dark Green and a tiny spot of Egyptian Red.
7. Practically all the colors were repeated in the apple, using very dark red "as is" for shadows, blended into Aqualon Yellow and dull Chartreuse for highlights.
8. The currants were of Burgundy, Garnet, Maroon and a bright red "as is" for highlights.

The bunch of green grapes was taken from the greens of the foliage, with the faintest touch of Aqualon Pink for highlights. Mrs. Borden had a wide variation of greens to choose from in developing the foliage. All materials were dyed over off-white, except those specified.

THIS ILLUSTRATION is from our first Western National Exhibit held in Masonic Temple Auditorium, Hollywood, Calif., Feb. 22, 23 and 24, 1951.

In the "Plume" (center), hooked by Barbara Rule of San Bernardino, Calif., Coe M. Green, Teacher, the intensity of color is applied to the corner leaf detail and the center background, being a moderate strength of Dark Green dye over light gray. The outside background is a blackish-green (strong Dark Green dye). The largest scrolls in the outer background are developed from grays of many values, and are heavily veined with green, using the darker values at the base, and flushing out to lighter values at the tips. The inside scrolls that form the border around the center are of weak intensities of varied greens, as follows: One edge changes from light tip to a dark base of blue-green, and that side of the scroll is filled with yellow-green. On the other side it is edged from light yellow-green to dark yellow-green base, and filled with blue-green. The veins are the grays of the outside scrolls.

The roses are of equal parts of Strawberry and Garnet in rather weak intensities. Lighter values of the same hues form the carnations. White lilies are shadowed with the grays from the large scrolls. The little small flowers that are clustered between the scrolls are of blues and lavender, with an occasional one of soft gold. Foliage around them repeat the greens from the smaller scrolls. Mrs. Green has very kindly kept a record of the amount of material used in this design, and graciously offers this information to you. The center background required 6½ pounds, the green scroll 3¾ pounds. The pupil kept track of her time and found she had put 1600 hours of hooking into her rug. It was her first rug!

The "Rainbow Border" (to the right of "Plume"), hooked by Ruby Grant of Detroit, Mich., Eleanor Aura Maxwell, Teacher, has an all black background, with one line of material that was spot-dyed with Cardinal, Olive Green and Yellow, that sets off the border. The floral detail is in an all-color harmony, from Cardinal, Purple, Burgundy, Yellow, Apricot, Peach, Copenhagen Blue, Violet, and foliage of yellow-greens, gray-greens, greens and blue-greens. The various intensities and values of the different hues enabled her to give each flower its own individuality.

The "Rainbow Border" (to the left of "Plume"), hooked by Helen Gifford of San Bernardino, Calif., Coe Green, Teacher, is of very similar coloring.

The "Rose Bower" (half round to the right) was hooked by Johnnie Mae Blakely of Corona, Calif., Teacher.

COUNTRY FAIR

You may wonder why many rugs are made by teachers, under the supervision of other teachers. It is a sign of growth, is it not, when we admit there is always something more to be learned from others?

"Country Fair," hooked by Claire Ashton, Teacher, of West Medford, Mass., under Sally Newhall, Teacher, was the result of saving just a little time out from classes for just such progress. She says: "Doing it gave me the biggest lift I have had for years, and so the rug is more than just a hooked rug. To me it is a personal triumph."

The fruit has been dramatized against an all black background. The plums and grapes which balance the ends and sides are developed from Purple, Plum and Mulberry dyes over white, with the addition of Copenhagen Blue in the grapes.

Pale yellow material was spotted with Terra Cotta and Burgundy for the peaches.

Varied yellows were spotted with Mulberry, Terra Cotta, Bronze and a touch of Olive Green for the pears.

Bright green materials were spotted with Old Gold and Bronze for the apples, and for an occasional transition to a colorful check, yellow material was spotted with weak Crimson.

Pale pink materials were spotted with Mahogany and a tint of Crimson for the cherries.

The strawberries were made from Cardinal over white. One end of a strip of white material was dipped about 2/3 of the way down into weak Olive Green dye, and the remaining end of the strip left white, to make a smooth transition for an unripe tip to some of them.

The currants (which were contained in a small area) were developed from four shades of rather bright red materials "as is."

The greens of the foliage varied. Some were made from bright green materials spotted with Olive Green and Taupe, others were of Reseda Green spotted with Rose, and still others were of yellow and very light blue materials dyed with Green. A blend of Greens was used for the peach leaves, and a blend of Olive Greens for the strawberry leaves.

Louise Lightfoot's Teacher Training Classes

IT IS quite common for teachers to take instructions from other teachers; or to join special Teacher Training Classes. Once a teacher creates a demand for her time, there is little opportunity to make many rugs.

When an advanced pupil is training for teaching, her main idea is to acquire as much experience in as short a time as possible. Thus, all those who are already teaching, or planning to, choose units of scroll patterns, samplers of geometrics, flower or fruit tiles, and chair seats on which to concentrate both technique and color. These units serve as visual aids in their own classes.

In the Teacher Training Classes conducted by Louise Lightfoot of Corona, California, Teacher, at Sister Kaddy McCabe's Studio in Sherman Oaks, the pupils were also taught to paint their detail on paper with the dye they were to use for their chosen colors. These paintings and their small hooked samplers were displayed at our Teachers' Fourteenth Annual Exhibit (1953). Those who participated in the display illustrated here are:

> Esther Foster of Long Beach, California
> Ditta Haas of Rialto, California
> Eva May Aud of Van Nuys, California
> Betty Weber of Los Angeles, California
> Marguerite Close of Los Angeles, California
> Marion Adams of La Crescente, California
> Gretchen Cohen of Los Angeles, California
> Orpha Romano of Long Beach, California
> Ruth Johnson, Santa Ana, California

Teacher Training Classes are not limited to the West Coast. In the East, Erline Stearns in Maine, Sally Newhall and Leona Lincoln in Massachusetts; Adrienne Bradley, Carolyn Collett and Myra Schwarzmeier in New York State; Phyllis Larsen in Washington, D. C.; and Frances Towe in New Jersey are a few of those who are continually bringing new ideas and fresh encouragement to the teachers in their areas.

There are as many different methods used by these teachers to instruct others as there are teachers. Some stress visual aids, some think the use of crayon sketches are very important, some begin with dyeing, believing that to be the first requisite in the process of creating beauty in a rug. The important thing is that they inspire other teachers to grow and expand so that all over the country there are women who are part of the web, bound together by those imaginary lines to which I previously referred.

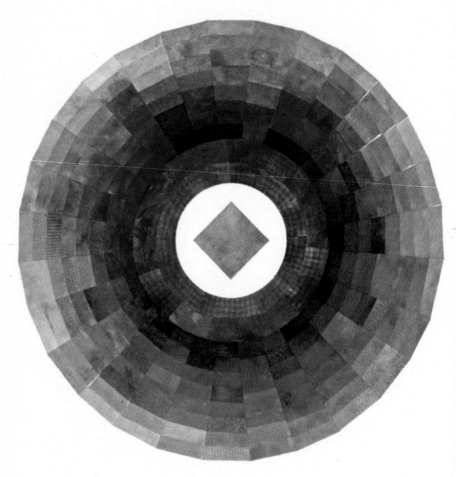

ALL-COLOR HARMONY DYE WHEEL

Notice in this all-color harmony that as you progress around the color wheel from RP–R to its complement, G–BG, and back again, the intensities are reduced and the values lowered.

This wheel was dyed for me by Alice J. Otis of Biloxi, Mississippi, Teacher, as a visual aid to show the freedom you may use in combining all hues in harmony, if they are in the right intensities. Thus, you are not bound in the use of color.

Mrs. Otis writes me: "I have been a great advocate of the fact that there is no *one right way* to paint a sunset or dye for a rug. Rather, there may be as many ways as there are people to employ them."

[284]

Teachers' Classes and Exhibits

Since the revival of this craft within the last two decades, a new vocation and a new field of endeavor have been opened up for thousands of women in all walks of life.

The sheer love of creative work has brought many women into the vocation of teaching the craft of hooked rugs, and their teaching has resulted in contentment and happiness to women who need a hobby to round out their lives.

Imagine invisible lines from this small town of West Boylston to all corners of this great country, for they do now reach into forty-three states — lines which reach into large cities and into small remote villages — lines which bind together the many, many women who are the teachers of this craft all over America. These teachers, too, have invisible lines reaching out in all directions toward those who are their pupils.

Ask any rugger what day she enjoys the most. Ten to one it will be her class day! Therefore, if there is any possible way for you to join a rug class conducted by one of my teachers, don't delay! You'll love it!

Classes are included in many of the Public, Vocational, and Evening Trade Schools. Oftentimes you will find them in the Y.W.C.A., Arts and Crafts Clubs, or under the auspices of the Home Department of Women's Clubs, or smaller private groups arranged by pupils and teachers. Ask me for the names of those nearest to you. I am always pleased to bring teacher and pupil together.

Getting away from home cares, worries and responsibilities for half, or the whole of a day, and being absorbed in this fascinating craft is a physical and mental benefit to you. The enthusiasm of fellow pupils, their interest in your work, and the helpfulness of the teacher in your own personal prob-

VISUAL AIDS BY ELIZABETH SPALDING, TEACHER

FROM THE time of my first Teachers' Exhibit I have been closely associated with Mrs. Elizabeth Spalding of Beloit, Wis. She was a teacher of Home Economic subjects in the Vocational Schools in Beloit, so it was not long before rug hooking became part of her class work. Her ability was recognized by the State Department of Education for she has since been training teachers throughout the state who meet annually for a State Teachers' Workshop.

In writing me concerning this illustration she says:

"A rug exhibit may be arranged with visual education in mind. Any information that points up a certain rug or group of rugs, the materials used, the type of dyeing, the source of color scheme, etc., is bound to make it more interesting and informative. In this group the students show their source of color scheme which might be a picture, piece of fabric, wallpaper, china, lamp base, or any work by an acknowledged artist.

" 'Lilium' (first left) has a complementary color scheme — taken from the Color Wheel. Purple-reds and purple-blues combined with soft gold and yellow-greens against a dark blue outer background and beige center. Mulberry dye was used for the many tones in the roses and grayed Mulberry formed the scroll. The veining and knobby parts of the scroll were done in green. The lilies and rose buds carried the soft gold and completed the harmony.

" 'Breath of Spring' (second from left) got its inspiration from a lovely Swiss print of crocus and pussywillows. The design was worked out in a split complementary scheme, red-violet, violet and violet blue, with gold and yellow-green forming a nice balance.

"The dramatic contrasts and rich coloring (burgundy and purple-blue on an off-white background) found in the hand-screened design of slip cover and draperies were repeated in 'Beth's Scroll' (third from left). The simplicity of the scroll in this design permitted the use of the same rich purple-reds that were used in the floral center.

" 'Summer Splendor' (fourth from left) is a bedroom rug done in warm yellow-reds like the chintz pattern in the wallpaper. While the coloring is warm and rich the creamy white background gives it a light almost fragile look. There is just enough blue used in the design to balance the old rose, maroon and soft golds."

"Lilium" hooked by Mrs. Elmer Wee
"Breath of Spring" hooked by Mrs. Randolph Hopkins
"Beth's Scroll" hooked by Mrs. Frank Brinckerhoff
"Summer Splendor" hooked by Mrs. Fred O'Neal

} Elizabeth Spalding, Teacher

COLOR TREE

lems make it a fruitful day. You may bring samples of wallpaper, draperies, or upholsteries and discuss your color plans personally with the teacher. You may turn to her when you have completed your dyeing for reassurance on your colors.

There is nothing that can take the place of this personal relationship between teacher and pupil, which extends beyond the sphere of instruction and advice. For there is always the human angle. Teachers are quick to sense the personal need or problem of a pupil, and help her achieve her desire.

I once heard Margaret Farnsworth (Teacher) say: "I would have lost interest in teaching the craft years ago if it was confined to mere instruction. It is what hooking does for pupils, and the changes which have come over people when they begin to hook, that makes teaching so satisfying."

Of course, the teachers have their problems too. A pupil is not always led to what a teacher may think is best for her.

Viola Shultz (Teacher) remonstrated with a pupil who said: "I know I should do a smaller rug first, but I am not going to. I am a retired school teacher and haven't long to live, and I am going to do what I always wanted to." And she did! Even Teacher was thrilled with the result.

Using color, which is so new to many pupils, and doing something of this kind for the first time in their lives is a revelation! It opens up a whole new world. They observe the work others are doing. From each they gain something new. Their real appreciation comes when the rugs are in their homes and a part of their lives. My mail is flooded with letters (and I DO love to receive them!) from pupils who write, unsolicited, of their affection for their teachers and the joys of hooking. So many say: "Why didn't I learn of this craft years ago? I've wasted so much time!"

What is this magic the teachers have? How did this group grow? Well, the answer to the first question is that teachers bring out the ability of the individual to create. There is something very satisfying in creating with color. As to the second question, it is like a fairy tale, and even the teachers themselves

IRIS J. WHEELER'S SUMMER RUG CAMP

A week's vacation at beautiful Green Lake in Spicer, Minn., is combined
with instruction and good fellowship in the Summer Rug Camp conducted
by Iris J. Wheeler and Alice Brown of Minneapolis, Minnesota, Teachers.

may not know all its history. Its growth really began to spread when Ruby Frederick, then of Winchester, Mass., carried her talent back to Michigan during a summer vacation, and encouraged Eleanor Aura Maxwell (then of Sault Ste. Marie, but now of Detroit, Mich.) to teach. Since then Mrs. Maxwell, or her pupils who have become teachers, have trained most of those who, at the present time, are teaching in that state.

At the same time, Mrs. Frederick interested Elizabeth Spalding of Beloit, Wisconsin, who was a teacher of Home Economics in the Vocational School there, and she has since trained most of the other teachers in Wisconsin.

Iris J. Wheeler of Minneapolis, Minnesota, was the pioneer who carried our technique to that part of the West. Coe Green of San Bernardino, California, was the first to take it back to the West Coast. Louise Battle of Memphis, Tennessee, was the first to become a traveling teacher through Tennessee and Arkansas and the upper part of Mississippi. In the deep South, Alice J. Otis of Pascagoula, Mississippi, was not only the first to introduce our technique in her area, but the first to train new teachers.

In the meantime, the number of teachers in the East, where we had the greatest activity, had been growing rapidly. Near home, Sally Newhall of Shirley, Mass., had always been closely associated with me, conducting classes in my home for many years. This gave me the opportunity of following closely the problems of all ruggers, and also work out some of my own ideas through her pupils, which I have passed on to thousands of interested people through my Letter Service and other publications. Those home classes at Rose Cottage have now had to give way to Teachers' Days, and Mrs. Newhall's own time is in demand for special Teacher Training Classes.

This vocation has been particularly appealing to women whose families are grown, and who are seeking an outlet for their energy; or those who, having lost loved ones, can only find comfort in doing something for others.

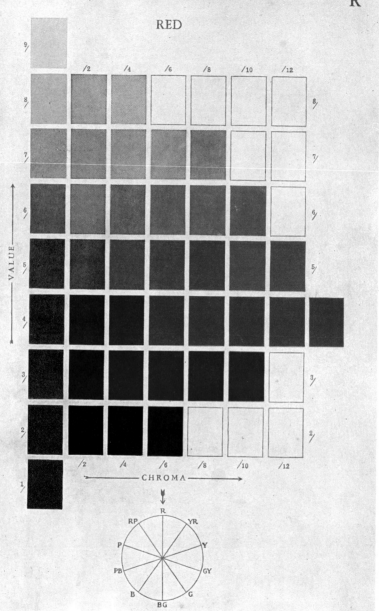

RED

PLATE OF RED (MUNSELL)

Plate of 5 Red by special permission of
Munsell Color Company, Inc., Baltimore, Md.

Like everything else, progress demands continuous growth, and even a good teacher has to keep on her toes to hold her following. Thus, women from various parts of the country have been eager to improve their abilities. Teachers who have become nationally recognized among ruggers for the special qualifications which enable them to prepare women for this vocation, conduct special classes for this purpose.

Teachers traveling about the country have carried the craft into new areas. Each teacher is a law unto herself, free to conduct her classes in her own way. Myrilla Ashley, who changes her residence frequently because of her husband's business, has not only started rug classes in Southern Pines, Charlotte, Davidson, and Mooresville, North Carolina, but, when their meeting place is large enough, invites others to bring their crafts and hobbies and join them for the day. The classes are called The Ashley Arts and Crafts Club, and when she leaves one residence for another, the Club is urged to go on meeting in the same way. Members in one location are encouraged to visit the Clubs in other cities, the meeting day always being Wednesday. What a wonderful way to leave something of yourself to benefit others!

Several years ago, when returning from California, I visited Greenville, South Carolina, and was invited by Dr. Peter Hollis, Superintendent of the Parker District Schools, to bring a group of my teachers to the Summer Camp of the School (Blythe Shoals), so residents of that district could have rug instruction. Since registration was open to residents of other areas, women from several surrounding states attended the first year. The Camp was conducted under the supervision of Claribel Harn of Greenville, S. C., Teacher, and has since become an annual event. For four years I co-operated with her, spending one to two weeks there each June. Since then, my teachers have continued to go on without me and have done a very creditable job. Many of the pupils who attended are now teaching. Other summer rug camps in other areas

BLYTHE SHOALS' SUMMER RUG CAMP

It was thrilling for me to visit with sixty-five pupils at Blythe Shoals (Camp Parker), and discuss their color plans as they hooked. The open pavilion was buzzing with activity. It was such a happy time!

have been a boon to those who desire to combine pleasure and instruction.

In July, 1951, the first PUBLIC Hooking Bee was staged on the green at Storrowton Village (Eastern States Exposition Grounds) in West Springfield, Mass. It was supervised by Mrs. Ione Winans, who had previously conducted three annual National Exhibits of hooked rugs in the Village. It brought over one thousand women to the green, with their frames, rugs, and lunches for the day. Several of my teachers joined me in short, helpful lectures, and gave demonstrations of dyeing. Since then Mrs. Winans has made it an annual event, and has started a demand for other Hooking Bees.

Most teachers, by the way, have their individual exhibits in their own locations, and these events are always publicized in my Letter Service, well in advance. Ruggers are very enthusiastic about attending these exhibits. Since most of them are held for the benefit of churches or charity, they have been a means of raising a tremendous amount of money for such purposes. I often wonder if the teachers themselves realize how much they have contributed for the common good of all.

Louise Hopfman of Lancaster, Mass., who several years ago graciously invited thirty-three of the teachers to spend a week at her home, for the purpose of exchanging ideas on hooking, was the founder of what later developed into the McGown Teachers' Workshop. As a result, it was extended to a two-week period in August each summer, and has since been held at the Atlantic Union College, South Lancaster, Mass., where we have had not only the use of several large and well-lighted classrooms, but the convenience of their school dormitories for living.

It is a teachers' co-operative organization, and I am happy to be a part of it in the capacity of Program Chairman. The intensive program includes lectures, the study of color, instruction on planning color through crayon sketches, developing visual aids to help them present their subjects to large school classes, as well as hooking. Every member must con-

[295]

HOOKING BEE — LENA MOSS, TEACHER

All through the summer many of the teachers have outdoor Hooking Bees for their classes, where the occasion becomes a day of sociability. Lena Moss (right) of Hudson Falls, N. Y., Teacher, entertains one of her classes.

tribute a lecture, demonstration, a finished rug or some visual aid which will help ALL teachers in their class work.

It is a happy time for all those attending. Women who have become mothers and grandmothers renew their school days attending classes, and living together in dormitories, form friendships which have given a new meaning to life.

But the highlight of each year is the Teachers' Annual Exhibit, which is always held for three days in May, in Horticultural Hall, Worcester, Mass.! Teachers representing forty-three states send three hundred fifty pupils' rugs for display.

The Exhibit is preceded by a Teachers' Conference before opening to the public. Thousands of visitors travel to Worcester to view the rugs and watch the demonstrations of this craft. The rugs illustrated herein are only a few of those which have been shown in these Exhibits.

VISUAL AIDS BY MRS. HOWARD L. SMITH, TEACHER

VISUAL AIDS awaken the interest of the uninitiated. In the illustration opposite, members of the classes conducted by Mrs. Howard L. Smith of Pascagoula, Mississippi, Teacher, have arranged visual aids on a long table, so that guests, upon entering the room, are confronted with a poster entitled "So you want to hook a rug?" Near by is a copy of my books "YOU . . . Can Hook Rugs" and "The Dreams Beneath Design."

Step #1 shows the selection of the design. Varied patterns are laid out so the details can be easily seen.

Step #2, a rug pattern is prepared for the frame, with a hemmed edge, and sewed half way down one side of the frame, with the needle and thread still attached, to show size of stitches.

Step #3, an arrangement of all kinds of wools, worn garments, and the typical collection a new rugger accumulates when she starts to hook.

Step #4, an arrangement of packaged dyes, dye solutions in quart jars, measuring spoons, cups, glass bowls, enameled pans, color charts and wheels, and copies of Dye Dabblers.

Step #5, the Cutting Machine with some of the material being fed through it, and the curved handled shears, a hook and burling iron. An arrangement is made of the cut material in neat, orderly manner, to show how to avoid confusion.

Step #6 shows a partially hooked rug on the frame, with strips of the various materials used in it, laid over the pattern so you may see the material before it is cut and hooked.

Step #7 shows the steaming or blocking of the finished rug, with the rug face down and a thick Turkish towel and a bowl of water, with an iron to complete the picture.

Standing with back to camera is Mrs. Otis with three guests.

Alphabetical List of Patterns

Name	*No.*	*Size*	*Publication*	*Page*
Acanthus Scroll	365	33 × 60		106
Agamenticus	442	36 × 68¼		216
Agatha Antique	157	30½ × 63		178
Amish	528	32⅝ × 50½	DD #37	250
Antique Leaf	251*	36 × 72	LS 5/49	178
Basket Weave	332*	37 × 83	DD #55	226
Beth's Scroll	274	30 × 42		286
Blue Heron	359	30 × 52		174
Blythe Shoals	590	32 × 56		112
Blythe Shoals	590	32 × 56		56
Breath of Spring	487	23¼ × 38	DD #15	286
Bridal Ring	565	35 × 59		176
Calla Lily Wreath	63	30½ × 58	DD #53–54	266
Cat's Paw	207†	24 × 36		224
Ceres	566	46¾ × 76	LS 11/51	124
Chilcott Leaves	191	36 × 68½	DD #39	106
Chilcott Runner	209	25 × 70½		92
Country Fair	584	36 × 60		280
Criss Cross	538	28⅞ × 46⅛	DD #50	48
Daphne	582 (pair)	28 × 46		238
Desire	570 (pair)	38¾ × 45		42
Dowry Needlepoint	541 (pair)	36½ × 62⅜	DD #49	122
Duke of Marlborough	532	34 × 60	DD #76	154
Early Americana	309	38 × 66½		232
Earth's Endowment	576*	28 × 45¾	LS 9/51	276
Eastland	113†	36 × 71½	LS 2/43	170
Elf's Delight	452	28 × 46		158
Entice	569	53¾ × 61⅝		220

*May be ordered in any number of motifs — any width or length.
†In more than one size.
LS — Subject of Letter Service — Issues available at 15¢ each.
DD — Subject of Dye Dabbler — Issues available at 25¢ each.

Name	*No.*	*Size*	*Publication*	*Page*
Farnsworth Scroll	81	46 × 77		154
Fascination	526*	24½ × 39½	DD #42	48
Filigree	567*	27 × 44⅛	DD #57	224
Fletcher Geometric	326*	35¾ × 69½	LS 5/54	260
Frost Oriental	134 (pair)	37 × 72		142
Fruit Scroll	316	31½ × 59½		238
Gainsborough	440	60 × 60		230
Gale Oval	99	38 × 60½		80
Garden's Gift	575*	28½ × 46¼	DD #69	120
Garden's Gift	575*	28½ × 46¼	DD #69	56
George Washington Scroll	363	38 × 72		110
Gifford Aubusson	238	34 × 58¾	DD #48	164
Gloria	586	74 × 87	LS 4–5/53	244
Goddess of Fortuna	542	45¾ × 95¾	LS 4/52	264
Harmony	537	30 × 48¾	DD #47	80
Harvest	444†	96 × 120		254
Hearts and Flowers	561A	60 × 96		94
Heart's Desire	517	20 × 40	DD #33	180
Hill's Leaves	338	30½ × 52	DD #30	212
Home in the Wilderness	595	22⅝ × 34¾	LS 9/53	258
Hot Irons	581*	40 × 62	LS 9/52	182
Jefferson Davis	608	46 × 80½		68
Key Border Oriental	138	32 × 54		208
Lagarza	276	40¼ × 56¼		262
Leaf Wreath	352	29 × 64¼		172
L'Faughnan	69	48 × 84		218
Lilium	460	29½ × 46		286
Little Middleboro	311	24 × 36		180
Lotus	572*	37½ × 60¾	DD #68	168
Lotus	572*	37½ × 60¾	DD #68	56
Lucetta's Tree of Life	591	57⅞ × 89¼	LS 11–12/54	248
Luseba	373	35 × 72		102
MacKay Scroll	288	34 × 66		172
Maltese Cross	154*	83¾ × 104⅛	LS 3/50	48

*May be ordered in any number of motifs — any width or length.
†In more than one size.
LS — Subject of Letter Service — Issues available at 15¢ each.
DD — Subject of Dye Dabbler — Issues available at 25¢ each.

Name	No.	Size	Publication	Page
Maltese Oriental	411	29½ × 50		48
Maturity	543	72 × 108		236
Maze Border	423A†	38 × 82½	LS 2/51	186
Mecca	598	47½ × 78¾		104
Memoria	560	40 × 80	DD #72–73	246
Memoria	560	40 × 80	DD #72–73	142
Miller Floral	304	50 × 67½		222
Mooney Pansy	153	30 × 48	LS 3/51	158
Norma Antique	355	24¼ × 46¼		176
North Star and Compass	379	36 × 72		216
Oak Leaves	8A*	56 × 80	DD #74	90
Oak Leaves Runner	8*	50 × 122	DD #74	170
Oak Leaves (Stair Runner)	354	28 inches wide, any length		188
Old Colonial	384A	75 × 100		150
Ollivia	398A†	55 × 96	DD #20–21	132
Omár Kháyyám (small size)	527†	44¼ × 68¼	DD #20–21	228
Open Flower	28	37½ × 65		200
Oriental Stair Runner	381	27 inches wide, any length		188
Perfume Box	492	29 × 54	DD #31	272
Persian Paradise	506	38 × 56		46
Persian Ribbon	498	27 × 49½		146
Plume	523	84½ × 84½		278
Plume	523	84½ × 84½		240
Polly	583	31½ × 46		48
Quaker	564 (pair)	36 × 64	DD #58	196
Queen's Desire	507	46 × 80		64
Rags to Riches	515	50¾ × 104	LS 3/54	44
Rags to Riches	515	50¾ × 104	LS 3/54	214
Rainbow Border	512 (pair)	38 × 78		278
Reed Oval	97	33½ × 60¼		88
Richmont Scroll	425	54 × 88		114
Rockland Scroll	431	28 × 50		146

*May be ordered in any number of motifs — any width or length.
†In more than one size.
LS — Subject of Letter Service — Issues available at 15¢ each.
DD — Subject of Dye Dabbler — Issues available at 25¢ each.

Name	No.	Size	Publication	Page
Romantique	441	34 × 60	LS 1/53	154
Rose Bower	433	23 × 37		278
Rugmaker's Song	473	20 × 33		242
Rustic Charm	551*	47½ × 71½		190
Scroll from "Symmetry"	548 Sp.‡	36 × 40		274
Sea Grapes	534*	30½ × 44½	DD #64	256
Season's Promise	500 (pair)	28 × 46	DD #25–26	76
Seven Sisters	503	33 × 55	DD #28–29	112
Southern Belle	520	34 × 60⅛	DD #67	274
Stained Glass Window	301*	32 × 62		204
Strawberry Patch	533*	27 × 43¾	DD #40	250
Summer Splendor	504	21 × 32		286
Sweetheart Rug	91	37 × 80		234
Sylvan Scrolls	446	54 × 88		122
Symmetry	548†	50 × 104		270
Thirteen Stars	366	21 × 33½		174
Thoughts of Love	577	35 × 60		252
Three Rose Oval	105	33 × 42		66
Treasured Shawl	472	30 × 48	DD #4	46
Twin Scotties	263	28½ × 49		66
Unity	605*	26 × 42	LS 4/54	184
Vermont Geometric	86*	29⅝ × 49⅜		170
Vermont Shell	59†	28 × 41	LS 10/53	268
Water Nymph	562	30 × 54		242
Watson Square	161C*	31 × 44¾		186
Whipple	344*	35½ × 54⅞		78
Wild Rose Lattice	20B	32 × 52		212
Winter Sunset	148	33 × 54		200
Woodland Sprite	563 (pair)	32 × 58	DD #62	136
Woodland Sprite	563	32 × 58	DD #62	170
Worcester Oriental	249	29 × 55		208
Young Man's Fancy	494 (pair)	24½ × 41	DD #51	142

*May be ordered in any number of motifs — any width or length.
†In more than one size.
‡Available on special order.
LS — Subject of Letter Service — Issues available at 15¢ each.
DD — Subject of Dye Dabbler — Issues available at 25¢ each.

List of Other Publications

PAMPHLETS

SO YOU WANT TO HOOK A RUG! . . . . $ .35

DYE PAMPHLET — beginner's dye instructions 35

THE RAINBOW IN RAGS — complete instructions for dyeing — a "must" for creating beautiful hooked rugs . . . 1.00

THE GIST OF GEOMETRICS — with 24 illustrations and suggestions for colors in 17 different designs 1.00

OBJECTIVES IN ORIENTALS — with instructions for each little motif and border in 9 different Oriental designs . 2.00

HELPFUL HINTS ON HOOKED RUGS — Illustrations of 45 completed hooked rugs 50

PICK AND CHOOSE — a descriptive list of my hooked rug designs (but not illustrated) 1.00

PETITES FOR PRACTICE — a descriptive list of chair seats, footstools, bags, tiles, pictures, table tops, pillow tops, and luggage straps (not illustrated) 50

COLOR COURSE — a correspondence course on COLOR, based on the Munsell system — including a set of 362 color swatches, and formulas to obtain each. Especially slanted toward the practical application of color to hooked rugs, including constructive criticism on two pieces of hooking 60.00

TRAINING FOR TEACHERS — fundamentals and principles of teaching, and ways of conducting classes — available only to my group of teachers 5.00

My books — "YOU . . . CAN HOOK RUGS" — the entire process of the technique of hooking rugs — 16 colored plates, 100 black and white illustrations of beautiful rugs, with descriptions 6.00

"THE DREAMS BENEATH DESIGN" — a story of the historical background of the old original and early American designs of hooked rugs, with many interesting stories concerning the rugs and those who made them. A delightful and authentic bit of Americana. A charming gift book — artistically designed and profusely illustrated 2.00

Recommended by the American Library Association